PLEASE DON'T INTERRUPT

Published in 2025 by

Griots Lounge Publishing Canada
www.griotslounge.ca
Email: info@griotslounge.ca

Please Don't Interrupt

This is a work of Literary Collections.

Library and Archives Canada Cataloguing in Publication

ISBN: 978-1-7383340-4-9

Cover and Interior Design by Sarah Peters, Galley Creative Co.

This project was funded by the Manitoba Arts Council.

MANITOBA ARTS COUNCIL CONSEIL DES ARTS DU MANITOBA

Printed and bound in Canada

Please Don't Interrupt

An Anthology

Edited by
Rona Altrows &
Uchechukwu Peter Umezurike

To our contributing writers

Contents

Introduction

RONA:

The theme of this book was sparked by a writing session. While drafting an essay, I noticed that the true story I was recounting pivoted on interruption. I began to reflect on the critical role of interruption in my life and after a while, I realized that my mental meandering had interrupted the essay writing I was supposed to be doing. My life was full of interruptions. Everyone faces interruptions, in one way or another, on a regular basis.

I saw potential for creative exploration of the idea of interruption through the development of an anthology. I wanted to hear from writers at different points in their careers and lives and I wanted diversity.

I also knew that I wanted a co-editor, and in a literal vision, I received confirmation of my instinctive sense that Uche Umezurike should be that partner. Fortunately for me, he agreed. With his poet's ear and quiet determination, Uche has taught me a lot in the course of the project.

UCHE:

On June 20, 2022, Rona Altrows emailed me about an idea she wanted to share. It was more than an idea; it was a vision. It was her vision of us working together on a literary project. I replied promptly. Then, she followed up with a phone call. Over the few minutes we spoke, I did not hesitate to identify with her vision because it was so compelling. I needed no further convincing. I knew she was a fantastic writer, and she would never relent in actualizing that vision. I wanted to be part of its actualization. Moreover, I had read her work, and I remain moved by the expansiveness of her social vision.

And the theme itself was captivating: "Interruption," which signals a break in action, a pause, an interval, and a cessation, albeit temporarily. To interrupt. To be interrupted. Following its Latin roots, the word itself indicates a break. For example, *inter* (between) and *rumpere* (to break). Interruption speaks to whatever is between the break, not necessarily a break. Imagine the "between" as a pause. The sigh or inhalation that interruption elicits from the one who has been interrupted by something, big or small. One of our book aims is to get readers to think more broadly about the "between" in their lives.

Life will never be bereft of interruptions. The consequences arising from one moment of interruption can be stressful and unsettling or heartwarming and revitalizing. This is another insight the book has offered me, one of the gifts I have gleaned from working with Rona in the past three years. It has been an exacting journey, but it has also been uplifting in many ways. It is a wellspring of delight and education, this journey! By delight, I mean I would not have read many poignant works by established and upcoming writers from across Canada if she hadn't made this opportunity available. Also, by education, I have learned so much from her thoughtful approach to editing and collaboration and her unstinting commitment to literature.

I might have been interrupted along the way, during the initial and final stages of putting the book together. But it has been fun. Yes, it has been worth every moment working on this beautiful *interruptio* of a book. Now, I hope you, our dear readers, will allow us to interrupt you with rhapsody over our book. As you sit with the pages, relish the "between" that interruption makes noticeable in today's world.

Daalu.

RONA AND UCHE:

Starting with the understanding that interrupting and being interrupted are universal human experiences, we sought out, as contributors, a diversity of writers, each with their own take on the theme. In *Please Don't Interrupt* we hear from writers who have immigrated to Canada from South America, from Africa, from Asia, from Europe, for a host of different reasons. We hear from writers living with debilitating illness, from older writers, from Indigenous writers, from Black writers, from writers who are survivors of trauma, from neurodivergent writers. We hear from writers at different points in their lives and in their writing careers. Some of our contributing writers' names may be known to readers. Other names may be new to readers and will become familiar over time as more of their work gets published.

Please Don't Interrupt is in seven sections, each of which focuses on a different aspect of interruption. Within the sections, contributing writers offer poetry, nonfiction, hybrid pieces, and fiction. Four prose pieces are fiction: "The Playhouse" by Wendy McGrath, in the section *KIN*; "The Many Voices of You" by Yejide Kilanko, in *MIGRATION*; "Little Love Songs" by Anna Marie Sewell, in *MINDWALKS*; and "Quicksilver," by Thea Bowering, in *REBUILDING*. All the other prose pieces are nonfiction.

It has been an honour to interact with all our contributors as they moved through the editing process. Professionalism, openness, and compassion exemplified this process. We have honoured the vision of each writer fully, including any deviations from standard English usage and punctuation that they deemed necessary to serve their works. Our contributing writers have showed commitment to the theme, trust in us as editors, and patience. Interacting with them and their work has made us better people. Every piece has made the book stronger.

Welcome to *Please Don't Interrupt*.

Acknowledgments

We are immensely grateful to our families, who have given us unconditional (and uninterrupted) support with this project at every stage, from conception to publication.

Many thanks to Griots Publishing Canada and especially to Griots Team Leader Bibi Ukonu, for his work and for his belief in *Please Don't Interrupt*. Bibi has been encouraging, responsive, and patient with us throughout the process.

KIN

Purey

Lenore Rowntree

I watch my sister Beth crossing the room. Her mouth is moving. Her mouth is pretty much always moving.

If Beth is in a quiet mood, you have to get up close to hear what she's saying. If you do, you'll hear something like this:

Grandma Rowntree and Saints. Aunt Helen and Saints. Saints. Faints. Gaints. Raints. Right! Hahaha. Sinners and Saints. Liars and Saints. Warfuls and Saints. Saints and Religions. Tearfuls. Missions. Hissions and Prissions. Now Dear… Ah Mary Hughes. Reethius Neethius. Magical Power. And that has nothing to do with Magical Powers. Magical Religious Power. Magical Father Ko Power… oh, don't you know Miss B, magical power. Magical power in livers. Magical powers in pancreases. Magical powers in bellies and pancreases. Bellies, pancreases, tissues and issues.

If you undo her words and include line breaks, they lie on the page like poetry.

Grandma Rowntree and Saints.
Aunt Helen and Saints.
Saints.
Faints.
Gaints.
Raints.
Right!
Hahaha
Sinners
……and Saints.

Beth has multiple soundtracks going in her head. She scats out only some of the voices she is hearing. In another life, she might have been a jazz singer.

When she is upset or someone has hurt her feelings, her speech is louder, more of a rant that goes like this:

Shouts! SHOUTS! SHOUTS! Oh no dear, don't shout. Yes, mistress you've been told. You're just a retard. A nut! Why thank you, NUTS GROW ON TREES. And trees are GRAND. Retards get out. Get out of our school. Miss Peters says GET OUT. Miss Lindsey says GET OUT. Donna Wanna says, retards and pretards. GET OUT. ALL GET OUT! Priests & Reverend East. Everyone join for the miracle crusade tour. HAHAHA, NO DEAR, NO MIRACLE CRUSADE FOR YOU. Pretty voice. Thinking of pretty voices. Avoid lies and rough teases. Ah, be quiet mistress.

Whether quiet or loud, a call-and-response goes on in whatever room Beth is in. When we were kids, it was as if some raucous version of the Tabernacle Choir wearing Dalmatian fur coats provided a soundtrack for the house. The Dalmatian coats are a nod to our favourite childhood character Cruella de Vil, and a reflection of just how absurd the scene was before Beth moved out into her first group home as an adult.

For most of Beth's seventy years, except when she is asleep, she has been nonstop talking. She's ingenious at figuring out how to keep the self-conversation going. It continues during movies, in church, and throughout every other conversation going on around her. It would not matter if the Prime Minister, Seth Rogen, Margaret Atwood and Salman Rushdie were all in the room trying to speak with her. She'd ignore them. She's a master at not being interrupted while at the same time interrupting everyone else. She rolls on, even when someone tells her to "shut up." Generally, she ignores a shut up, too. Sometimes she will slip in an "I will not shut up," then without skipping a further beat, she'll get right back to whatever list she is firing off.

Beth wakes up talking. It starts with a mumble when she is lying in bed half-awake in her nightgown. Bear nightgowns were once a favourite, currently French bulldogs festoon her nightwear. The talking continues from her bed to the bathroom. If left unchecked, it will get louder and punctuated with laughter as she pulls on whatever pants and t-shirt were left on her chair the night before. She does try to remember to put on deodorant and brush her teeth, but that doesn't always happen. Hand lotion, though, and lots of it, will happen whenever it is available. It's not for lack of trying that she doesn't get dressed properly. Beth wants to do good, to be good. It's just that everything in her life is a huge effort. When pressed, she puts it simply, "My life is hard, you know."

If you ask her what else she might want to wear other than the clothes from the previous day, she will say, "Pretty makeup and a dress." Given a choice of outfits, she always chooses the most colourful—a blueberry coloured blouse, a psychedelic carrot-lime swirl skirt, sparkly rainbow beads, and a pearl-studded headband. The result, except for the orthopedic shoes, looks a lot like a juice box.

She can't help the talking. She lives with an undefined and apparently undefinable mental illness. Hers may be a dual diagnosis of autism and childhood-onset schizophrenia, or it may be brain damage from a difficult birth, or it may be something that's not yet in the psychiatry textbooks. The psychiatrists, of whom there have been many, cannot agree, and we are past trying to figure it out, as she is pretty much drug-resistant to any treatment she's tried. Yet she still takes a daily fistful of medication. Most psychiatrists, especially in the terribly underfunded public mental health system in British Columbia, work primarily by prescription pad. It's quick and it's cheap, and it's somebody else's problem to procure the tablets.

Some of her psychiatrists think Beth's talking is a self-soothing technique. They may be right. For sure, it's a distraction from the multitude of things buzzing through her head. I feel terrible that she has to live with this affliction, whatever it is. My sense of it is that she is wired to the universe. All the currents of life are funneled into the top of her head, and from there they course through her mind at hundreds of miles per hour with no outlet except her mouth.

Neologism (made-up words) and word salad speech patterns are hallmarks of schizophrenia. Beth definitely makes up words and she likes her word salads well tossed, so a tick under the column for schizophrenia. One of her psychiatrists says until she met Beth, she had never known anyone with the ability to be living in psychosis and in the real world at the same time. You can interrupt Beth during one of her rants to say, "Beth I need you to listen," and right between "Reethius" and "Neethius" she will say, "Yes. Are we going for coffee?" then get back to her list. Listing is a symptom of autism, so a tick under that column.

Reethius and Neethius are some sort of shorthand for all religions and nationalities, the elements of which I am unclear about. Beth's meaning may change from time to time, although she has been using these words for decades. The wonderful thing about made-up words is that the maker always has, in his or her mind, the perfect word for the occasion. And there is never any end to the words that can be used. The other day, Beth said, "And Beethius, too." When I asked her what Beethius means, she said, "Bibles," and when I asked why she didn't just use the word "bible", she said, "It's different," and gave me that quizzical look like how could I not know that.

The Playhouse

Wendy McGrath

1

– I built that goddamn playhouse, and it just sits there in the backyard.
– She's too old for it now.
– She is only ten.
– Going on eleven.

Leo shook his head, blew smoke over the table in his wife Bev's direction. He stubbed his cigarette between the handles of the crossed knife and fork on his empty plate and pushed it away.

– Should've built it five years ago, before she gave up asking you. Too late now. You don't see what's going on right under your nose. You just don't see.

Secretly, Leo knew that. He realized too late that the time for a playhouse had passed and that he had built it to cover up his lack. Misplaced amends. Leo also knew his wife didn't always know what was going on right under *her* nose. "Measure twice, cut once," that's what Leo said. Leo always measured twice, but he cut more than once on more than one occasion.

Before Leo built the playhouse, their sea-foam green Galaxy 500 was parked on the concrete pad that would one day be covered by the garage. Insulated and with power so he could plug in the car in winter. Right now, though, the garage was just a suggestion, a wooden frame that looked like those first lines his older daughter Robin pressed into paper when she drew a building. The garage would be tucked between an open space in the fence just wide enough for the driveway.

One Saturday, Leo had been working on his own house, not pouring concrete, or framing, or building for someone else. He had been cutting 1x4s in the basement. Framing-in the rumpus room. He had a length of 1x4 in his hand when he saw Robin at the top of the basement stairs.

– Dad.

It was the way she said it, quiet, just pointing toward the backyard. Leo took the basement stairs by two and ran around the corner of the house, the hammer in his tool belt hitting the side of his leg with each stride. All four doors of the green Galaxy were flung open, and inside the car was a snarl of movement. There was an ungodly yelping, and he could hear his younger daughter, Fran, screaming but couldn't see her. Leo saw the German Shepherd. In flashes the big dog circled the backseat with the dachshund Dash in its mouth, shaking him side-to-side so fast the little dog looked like it was melting.

– Sonnuvabitch.

Leo ran toward the car, focused on the shepherd, still holding the 1x4. When the shepherd jumped from the car with the small dog still clamped in its teeth, Leo lifted the 1x4 and swung it with all his strength over the shepherd's skull. The board broke in two. The shepherd dropped, eyes still open, tongue hanging out, blood beginning to seep out its mouth. The dachshund lay on his side, whimpering and shivering beside the car. He was bleeding from his haunches, the blood soaking his smooth brown fur, so that now it looked as if he was wearing one of those fancy coats rich people put on their dogs. Leo stood with a bloodied piece of wood in his hand.

– Fuck.

2

Leo had always had a knack for imagining things in places where there was nothing before. He also discovered he had a knack for building those things and for the sheer hard work that needed to be done to make those things real. On the job site he kept his mind occupied by focusing on multiplying hours worked X hourly wage = paycheque. Pounding nails, he recited "The Wreck of the Hesperus" silently to the rhythm of his hammer.

Leo thought he was smart. He had gone to a one-room schoolhouse. Not the romantic, nostalgic little red schoolhouse people make stories up about where a matronly, but kind, schoolmarm in a black dress and white collar stood in the doorway and rang a huge bell for the poor, yet happy, farmers' kids, letting them know it was time for school. The picture he remembered was of fifteen kids from grades one to nine and a young woman, no, a girl, not much more than a kid herself, in front of a chalkboard. Looking back, he realized that she would probably have been from some one-horse town and gotten her teacher's certificate billeting with some family in Saskatoon, maybe Regina. When the teacher saw how smart Leo was and how quickly he finished the work she gave him, she panicked and put him ahead two grades. To keep him occupied, she had him learn by heart "The Wreck of the Hesperus" (she had first read it in teacher's training) and recite it in front of the class.

But jumping two grades did not make a happy equation for Leo's math, or chemistry, or physics—such as those sciences were, or could be, taught by that green, young teacher in that pokey one small room. He was lost. He was convinced he had suddenly turned stupid. He quit school in grade ten and moved to Prince Albert. Got a job pouring basements and moved up to framing houses. No one could hammer-in a mouthful of nails faster than he could. Two hits on the head. All it took to pound that sucker down.

3

Robin stood over Dash. He tried to lift his head, then dropped it back down on the ground. She was afraid to touch him and stood there unable to speak. Her younger sister, Fran, was still crying in the front seat of the car. Her dad dropped the broken piece of wood he had in his hand and, to Robin, seemed to fly to the car, lift Fran out of the front seat and take her inside the house. Her dad came back to Dash and Robin with a blanket and wrapped it around the dog. Dash yelped as her dad gently lifted him off the ground.

– What are we going to do, Dad?

– We'll take him to the vet, 'kay? He'll be fine. He's a tough little weiner.

– Her dad patted her on the shoulder.

– Do vets work Saturdays?

– We'll check the phonebook.

– Or call Information? Robin offered. The little dog whimpered.

– Yeah, Information.

Robin ran ahead of her dad and opened the back door for him and Dash. At the top of the stairs, her mother held a still-blubbering Fran. Her dad brought Dash inside, placing him gently on a pile of his work clothes, crumpled in a corner of the porch. Dash shivered.

– Leo, you'll get blood on…

– Bev.

Robin thought how strange it was to hear her parents calling each other by their first names.

– Keep the kids in.

4

Leo closed the door behind him, headed back out to the yard. The shepherd lay where it fell. Leo took his hammer from his tool belt and held it up, his work boots feeling heavy as he slowly walked toward the dog. The shepherd's eyes were open, the blood pooled around its head like a halo. Leo nudged the dog's back with head of the hammer. The dog was dead.

5

Robin watched her dad building the playhouse and made a point of not laughing at the jokes he made as he worked.

– I'm busier than a cat shoveling shit on a cement floor. Bluer than a cross-eyed carpenter's thumb.

She saw her dad create a square wood frame floor from a few 2x4s. He framed the walls leaving openings for a small door and window, pitched the roof, nailing on the sheets of plywood. He shingled the roof and painted the whole playhouse with bright coral paint left over from painting this new house in the new neighbourhood. He finished the playhouse one spring weekend. In the mornings, the grass was still cold on the north side of the house.

– It took you one weekend. You could've built it when we moved in.
– Christ, Bev, I've built it now, haven't I?
– Why do I always have to tell people to do things over and over? Why can't people just do what I tell them when I say it the first time?

6

Alone inside the playhouse, Robin realized she really didn't "play" anymore. She had never played made-up games from scratch anyway. That was Frannie's talent—she could carry on conversations with her plastic horses for hours at a stretch. Robin jumped out the door and stood beside Leo outside the playhouse. Both crossed their arms over their chests.

– Dad, could you make some kind of trap door with a secret passage in this thing?

Robin imagined lifting a door in the playhouse floor. The kitchen floor in their old house had a door that Robin's mother had lifted with a big ring. It opened to the dirt basement where the wringer washer was. Robin didn't want a dirt basement under the playhouse. She wanted the trap door to lead to a maze of tunnels underneath their new neighbourhood.

– You watch too much TV.

– It would be fun, Dad!

– Where would a trap door go to?

– Well, you could dig a tunnel somewhere?

– Highly unlikely, her father laughed, reached into his shirt pocket for his cigarette pack.

– Okay, I'll dig it then.

Leo plucked a cigarette from the pack as if he were taking a nail from his tool belt. He put the cigarette in his mouth. "Another coffin nail," he said. Leo reached for a pack of matches from the front pocket of his jeans and lifted the flap. There was a phone number written inside, but Robin couldn't see the name. Robin's parents had told her to memorize her address and phone number in case she was ever kidnapped. With visions of herself being snatched off the street, tied up and thrown in the trunk of a car, she had memorized her address and phone number, writing it on the back of her drawings and on the pages of the stories and poems in the scribbler she never showed anyone. Now she tried to memorize all the phone numbers she could—her grandparents', her aunt's, her piano teacher's, her friends'—just in case no one was home to answer the phone when she escaped from being kidnapped. She could call all the other numbers until she found someone who could rescue her. If she had enough phone numbers memorized, eventually, she would get someone on the other end of the line. Leo lit his smoke and took a big drag, shaking out the small flame and throwing the spent match on the grass. The tip of the cigarette glowed red, like those little match heads.

– Whose phone number is that, Dad?

– Huh?

– I saw a phone number on the inside of your matches. Whose is it?

– Uh, the plumber. I'll get you a shovel, he said, smoke punctuating his laughter.

7

The inside of the empty playhouse smelled like Robin's real house when it had been brand new, right after her father had built it. A clean, hopeful, happy smell of wood and fresh paint. She couldn't really remember her parents being happy a lot of the time when they lived in the old house, but they did laugh sometimes at TV shows. Robin would hear her mother shouting and her father shouting back and then stretches where they said nothing to each other. Her mother said the new house would be a fresh start. Robin felt proud when she told her friends her dad had built their new house himself.

The plywood floor of the playhouse had a bit of give. I could dance on this, she said to herself and bounced a bit up and down. Perfect for a go-go. She wiggled her hips and circled her arms. How many dances did she know? The swim. The hitchhiker. Easy. You just had to stick your thumbs out while you wiggled your bum. She would never hitchhike in real life, though. Her mother had told her that girls who hitchhike and take rides from strangers end up in ditches without arms and legs. Also dead.

Maybe she could just bring a book into the playhouse and read. She would have to bring a blanket for the floor, though. Dancing or reading. She could use the playhouse for those things. Or start a club. The club could raise money for Lotta Hitschmanova and the Unitarian Service Committee, but whenever she asked her mother if they could donate to Lotta Hitschmanova's committee, she said they were broke and didn't have any money to waste. Maybe Robin would just invite two friends over to the playhouse. Then they could decide what to do with it.

8

When Leo brought Dash back from the vet, his haunches were wrapped with white bandages.

Leo made Dash a kind of nest from the blanket Robin had used to make a tent against the fence. There were holes in the corners where she'd pounded them into the ground with broken clothespins. Leo arranged the blanket on top of an old, lumpy pillow in the back porch.

– Can I give Dash a hug? Robin asked

– I wanna give him a hug too, Francis said.

– No, leave him alone. The vet gave him a shot, something to make him sleepy so he won't move around and hurt himself.

– Will Dash be okay, Dad?

– He'll be fine. I told you, he's a tough little weiner. The vet said tomorrow we have to change the pads under that bandage there and start putting on some salve once a day. He has to have these pills twice a day.

Leo reached up to pass the bag of pills and ointment to Bev who stood on the top step. She mouthed:

– What did you do with the Shepherd?

– Finished the job, Leo said out loud.

– What job, Dad?

– Nothing. Never mind.

9

Her dad crouched beside Dash. Still in his work boots, laces undone and tongues flapping, still wearing work clothes. He stroked Dash's head, and the dog closed its eyes. Robin thought he looked so big next to their little dachshund curled quietly on that blanket, he seemed to take up the whole back porch. When Leo had carried Dash in from the car, for a moment Robin had thought that man wasn't her father. The way he had carried the small, white, paper bag, the way he had placed Dash so gently on the bed he'd made in the back porch. Still kneeling by the dog, Leo looked up at his wife.

– It could've been one of 'em.

When did you lose the power of speech?

Rona Altrows

I was pregnant, teaching high school English. I liked how the baby's movements seemed so often to complement my mood, as if she were my sidekick. My students were great. As for my colleagues, about half seemed open-minded, while the others struck me as pretty rigid thinkers. A math teacher, Tom, had daily questions for me in the staff room at the end of the lunch hour, when many teachers were around, preparing to return to class. In a tone that was conversational but loud enough for all to hear, he would say, How's the baby treating you today? Is the baby giving you grief? Then he'd fabricate a smile.

Those questions, his manner, made me sick, but I never answered. What was the point? I knew that behind my back, he made it clear to colleagues that he disapproved of pregnancy outside of marriage. He also expressed often, but never in my presence, a prurient interest in the identity of the father, which, for my own reasons, I had not disclosed. The open-minded colleagues liked me lots more than they liked Tom, so they kept me informed of his moral pronouncements and frequent speculations. I learned that Tom had even hosted a wine-and-cheese for colleagues he considered sympathetic to his position, to see if they could solve the mystery together. Could the father be someone they knew? And why wasn't I telling?

I wished that Tom's daily questions for me and his surreptitious dad-probe were not affecting me. After all, I knew he was mean and hypocritical. I also knew that the colleagues I respected were on my side. So why did I feel like my core was rotting?

I started obsessing over the issue. And that's what I was doing, silently, on a visit with my parents one Sunday evening. We sat, ate, talked politics, but the whole time my mind was at school, with the Tom problem. Once the meal was done, my mother looked at me and said, So, what is it?

I thought I'd been successfully covering up my feelings and thoughts, but once a mother calls a daughter out on her concealment game, that game is up. So I let it out. I told her about Tom, his lunch-hour questions and his sick private investigation. I told her I had kept quiet because I was afraid people would think I was overreacting, afraid I would sound as if I thought I'd done something wrong, even though I knew I hadn't. Afraid afraid afraid. Why should I call attention to his sneakiness, his twists, his attacks framed as expressions of concern? Wasn't my keeping silent a statement in itself? But what was that statement, exactly? Beset by misgivings, doubts, fear in its many guises, I was stuck.

My mother listened. What I noticed most was the position of her hands. Usually, when we spoke, her hands were busy, lifting a roasting pan from the oven or ironing a shirt. Tonight, those hands sat at rest on her lap.

When I was done, there was a pause. We were not a family of pausers, not when we talked to one another. We were interrupters. We even interrupted interruptions.

But my mother's pause continued. She kept her eyes fixed on mine. She did not look sad, worried, or angry—she looked inquisitive.

And then, this:

When did you lose the power of speech?

Um...

Roncha. Did I raise you to put up with crapola?

And that was it. I started to formulate a plan.

The baby moved. Not a kick. A shift.

Crawling

Dustin Archibald

I watch him as he kicks the ball, the coach/goalie stretching futilely to stop it from going in the goal. The ball tumbles through the air, past the goalie's outstretched hands, and sinks into the net with a soft *thump*. The boy jumps, cries the high-pitched celebration scream only children seem to make, that siren scream you dread as a parent the instant before you realize it means joy. The children behind him jump, whoop, and holler, ignoring the line the coaches have tried to corral them in. The coach in the goal drops to the ground, ready to perform five push-ups, his penance for letting the ball into the net.

Someone bumps my leg, and I look to my left to see a woman waiting impatiently for me to stand up from my seat so she can get past. I stand, the hard, plastic seat lifting on its springs. At least I get a moment's break from its numbing powers.

When she's gone, I turn back to the soccer pitch. The coach has finished his push-ups, and my son now stands at the back of the line, anxiously waiting for his next chance to score.

He's smaller than the other children, but that's all right. I was a small child too, and now I tower over most people. If his crooked teeth are any indication, he shares many of my genetic dispositions.

He waves vigorously at me, and I raise my hand back. He takes a drink from his water bottle, water spilling down his uniform. He doesn't notice. Instead, he tosses the bottle aside and starts flapping his arms like a chicken. Soon all the other children are doing it.

I would shake my head, but this is supposed to happen. It's the way it's supposed to be.

I made that resolution when he was born, when I was cradling him in my arms late at night, rocking him to sleep in front of the TV while

Wings reruns played on Netflix. I told myself that no matter what, I'd see him as he was, not as I wanted him to be. That as he grew up, I wouldn't wish for him to be a baby again. Or a toddler. Or a preschooler. I wouldn't try to hold on to the past-him. Instead, I'd live in his moment, with him as he was, no matter his age.

I think some of the best lies are the ones we tell ourselves.

That's not white hair, it's a trick of the light.

I'm not out of shape, it's this mirror.

I don't mind his growing up, that's the way it's supposed to be.

When you find out you're going to be a parent, people give you advice you don't want yet desperately need. Parents, young and old, convey wisdom passed down through generations of dirty diapers, sleepless nights, and skinned knees.

"Say goodbye to sleeping in."

"Better think about siblings before he gets too old."

"The days crawl, but the years sprint."

What they don't tell you is how desperately you'll try to claw back those years, holding on to scraps of memory weathered by time and stress. There are reasons the days crawl: there are screaming fits and nights spent lying beside him, wondering if the coughs and quick breathing are something more than mild croup. The jolt of irritation when someone rings the doorbell just as he gets to sleep. The rush to work, then the rush back home to give his mother a desperately needed break.

Surely that can't be all, though. Maybe my brain has blanked it out so I'll try to rein in the years, an evolutionary trick.

But I do remember some.

He's a toddler and we try to teach him not to pull the fur of the dog, a miniature poodle already old for a dog. "Gentle hands," we say as he clamps onto her with tiny, unfathomably strong fingers. Sometimes she nips at him, and we call that natural consequences. Of course, he doesn't care for natural consequences, and he never quite gets the concept of gentle hands. Instead, he prefers to keep his distance.

I take him to daycare on his first day. They had a meet-and-greet with the staff the day before, so he could get used to it. If you ever want your heart ripped out, take your child to daycare and, after saying goodbye, leave him there. Turn your back on someone who has consumed your every waking and sleeping hour and don't turn around. When you hear his cries because he realizes you're gone, just keep walking. Get in your car or truck or SUV and just go to work and leave that part of you behind, crying for you to come back. I don't know what's worse, that they don't want you to leave, or that they so quickly get used to your being gone.

By the time he's in kindergarten he's used to not being with his mom and me all day. I walk with him the few blocks it takes to get to school, his small hand clasped in mine. We skip over cracks in the sidewalk, his intensity for the game something I can never match. I mosey in a state of contemplative alertness, the continuous stream of his words accompanying my anxiety as we approach intersections. He doesn't stop, he talks and walks even if cars approach. He doesn't know how utterly stupid most drivers are. I need to teach him every time we walk. We get to the four-way stop and I remind him to make sure all the cars have stopped. Make sure people see him. Make sure to be safe. We cross the first road to the sidewalk, then wait to cross the other road. I remind him of everything I just said. He nods, but I'm not sure he gets it.

When we get inside the school, we find his cubby and he hangs up his backpack. He puts on his indoor shoes, ones with Velcro straps, because tying laces is too complicated. He gives me a hug and disappears into his room without looking back. I walk home alone.

When the pandemic hits, no one knows what to do. Everything shuts down, including schools. Of course, he has virtual daily interaction with his classmates, but that's not quite the same. There is a makeshift skating rink across the street in the park, one of the few things that hasn't been shut down. In the afternoons I get him dressed in his snow gear: ski pants and jacket, boots, mitts, and that knitted monkey hat he loves to wear. We trudge through the crisp snow to the ice rink, our breath whisked away on a quiet breeze. We bring his green plastic Ninja Turtle sled. Mounds of snow have been pushed by a skid-steer to the far sides of the rink. He climbs to the top of one mound, sets himself on his sled and zips down, bouncing all the way, sliding on the ice, his feet up in the air. He insists I take a turn. I slide much farther than he does, though I also get more snow down my pants. I never seem to learn to put on my ski pants.

We are shocked when those mounds are bulldozed over, victims of fluctuating pandemic unease.

He's older and wants to walk to school by himself. He's still too little. We compromise and agree that he can walk from the four-way stop to the school. Most drivers are stupid, but when it comes to four-way stops they are utterly useless. These are the same people who complain about getting photo radar tickets, as if there is no way to avoid them.

We take him to the Edmonton Symphony Orchestra Star Wars night. He loves Star Wars. The epic starship and lightsabre battles echo in our house almost daily. Edmonton downtown parking is atrocious, so we opt to park our car in a parkade and take the LRT. He's never ridden it before, the experience a wonder. We coach him on how to find the right train, how to stay away from the yellow line at the edge of the platform, how to push the button to open the door. He sits opposite us, our shoes gently bumping into each other as he talks.

The night is as magical for him as it is for me. The themes of Star Wars sing out in the theatre as I hearken back to my own childhood, watching Star Wars in the dark with my parents.

We board the LRT late at night and he sits facing us again, his back to the door. Then I see them: four young people, obviously drunk, their bodies no longer fully under their control, bottles of vodka tucked under their arms. Inside they stumble, three yelling at the first to enter, asking her to come back. She wears a grey hooded sweater and has been crying. She stomps past us, the harsh smell of alcohol wafting after her. The others follow, yelling at her to stop. The LRT doors shut, and the train begins to move.

I hear them behind me, a couple of rows back, laughing, their speech slurred. I get up and move beside my son. To keep an eye on them. One of them gets up and then the train slows, which causes him to drop his vodka and fall to the floor, spilling alcohol.

My son presses closer beside me and asks what's wrong with them and I say I'll tell him later. Even intoxicated people can have good hearing.

We arrive at our stop and exit, but then, so do the four. We take the stairs, and they follow, their raucous presence driving us on faster.

When we get to the parkade, we need to wait for a security guard to open the door. My wife stands by the door, I gently push him in front of her, so he is between us. I watch the four stumble and scream, kicking garbage. The one in the grey hood stands in the middle of the road, blocking the path of a bus as she swears and slaps the window.

The security guard comes, and I herd my son through the door. It'll be a long time before he understands how alcohol can do that to a person.

The day comes. We walk and I remind him of what he needs to do: wait for all the cars to stop, make eye contact with the drivers before you walk, and cross quickly but safely. We get to the four-way stop and he gives me a hug. He turns and waits for the vehicles to stop, then with his hand raised, walks quickly and confidently to the other sidewalk. A jacked-up truck on too-big tires approaches, exhaust billowing out its muffler. An idiot with far too much money and not enough brains. My son waits patiently for the truck to stop, and for a wonder, it does. He raises his hand and crosses the second street, calmly but swiftly, and then he is across. He waves at me, and I wave back. The bellowing truck guns it and tears across the intersection. If I had a rock, that truck would have one fewer window. When the truck is out of sight, I see my son round the corner to his school. I walk home alone.

I pass by his room at night to find it a disastrous mess. He has thrown all of his blankets to the floor and, apparently, half the clothes he owns. How someone so small can create such a large mess, I'll never understand. I step gingerly into the room, tiptoeing as if it is a minefield. He has replaced his blankets with books, hugging their bent pages to his chest like stuffed animals. I move the books and rescue the blankets from the floor, covering him once again. His breathing is steady. I shut off the light and close the door.

I now only walk a block with him before he goes out on his own to school. But then, one day, we get a phone call. He didn't show up to class, the office says. I ask if they're sure. Maybe they missed him. No, they say. He wasn't there when they took attendance.

When they hang up, I immediately call his mother at work. We make plans. She'll come home right away. Whose place would he go to? There's no one on the way. Could he have gotten lost? We've walked the same route countless times.

We don't speak our deepest worries.

I was wrong. If you want your heart ripped out of you, *this* is how you do it.

I'm halfway out the door when the school calls again. He's in class. He came in after attendance was taken and didn't check in at the office. I make another call to his mother.

We pick him up after school and ask him, what happened? Why was he late? He says he wanted to do a lap around the school before going to class and it took him a while. It makes sense, to him. I need to walk with him to school again. Until he doesn't get distracted.

They never warn you about that part, do they? The ones with all the advice. They tell you about the time you got lost in the store, even though you were only one aisle away, hiding in the clothes rack because it was dark and cozy. They joke about how they went out of their minds trying to find you, only to have you show up right where you should be, oblivious to their plight. They don't tell you about all the things that went through their heads. They don't tell you because it would only scare you. They don't tell you because it scared them. Everything turned out fine, after—

I feel a tap on my leg and I turn. There he stands, sweat dripping off his forehead, his cheeks flushed. The practice is over, and I've missed most of it.

"What are you doing, Dad?" he asks.

His eyes are wide, black hair plastered to his face. He wouldn't understand. That's the way it's supposed to be.

So I lie. The best lie.

"Nothing," I say.

We pack up his things, put his soccer shoes and his water bottle in a bag and, hand in hand, walk home.

Draw a Breath

Madelaine Shaw-Wong

A sledgehammer to the chest knocked the breath from my lungs. A phone call from your high school counsellor. She said you wanted to kill yourself.

Sweet Jesus, let it not be so.

A hurried drive to the school, and I gathered you in my arms. My sensitive, intelligent daughter. My child. Why the self-loathing? Why the despair? I love you. I said it repeatedly, a mantra, hoping the words would guard against the monster's torments.

I didn't understand, but I could hold you. I drove you to appointments. I bought your medications. I prayed. But I couldn't reach you when you were far away, a prisoner of your overwhelming sorrow.

The counsellor said you had already tried. I didn't know that. It was my turn for self-reproach and fear. I had failed to protect you, to understand that your pensive manner was more than teenage moodiness.

I kept guard at night, rising frequently from my bed to put my hand in front of your nose. Didn't care if I never slept again if I could keep you safe. Your warm breath was a temporary reassurance. Your sleeping face calm and worry-free, like the little child I remembered.

Moments of your childhood, sweet and powerful memories. I longed for those simpler times. Holding your tiny body on my chest, warm and wet with amniotic fluid. The toddler, spunky and curious, walking at ten months, talking soon after. My climber, forever in need of rescue from tables and counter tops. Sharing your childhood passions with me—books, bees, and pop stars.

You came home from school, upset. Some boys had bullied you. Such thoughtlessness and cruelty are unfathomable to sensitive people like you and me.

You fell in love, giving that tender heart away to ones who didn't deserve you. Your broken heart broke mine because we are tied, mother and daughter, by an unbreakable bond.

I took your hand, not allowing you to remain in bed. We walked in the sunshine. I encouraged you to eat, to talk, to exercise, to live.

You climbed into my bed one night and cried for help. The monster was on the loose again.

A night in the hospital. You in your new flannel pyjamas. We were lucky a room was available. I was wearied, though, by the battle. If I went home, if I rested, would I get a terrible phone call from the hospital later? You smiled, said no, you'd be okay.

Where did you go? When will you come back? Will you come back? The thought of losing you tore at my heart. I cried to friends, family, doctors, and clergy. Every tear a plea.

I begged—Lord, protect my child.

You did return to me, and for that I'm grateful. But will you be forever susceptible to the monster's claws and its terrible wide mouth that would swallow you up?

Perhaps, but you are tenacious and now better prepared to face life's troubles. I finally draw a breath.

MIGRATION

Immigrant Interruptions

Kelly Kaur

Part 1: Secret Arrival

The plane finally touches down on Singapore soil. The unexpected agony rises and lodges in the craw of my neck. I try to restrain hot, burning tears, but it is futile. It seems that the anguish of interruptions has intensified over the 37 years despite the countless visits I have made home. Maybe, it is the silent knowing that each excited anticipated hello will be met by a poignant, excruciating goodbye.

Maybe, it's because thoughtless time has hustled by with little regard for the missing chapters of our lives, for the unbeknownst permanent ache of absence, for the sorrow of unforeseen deaths of friends and family, for the distant joy of new family additions heralded through social media, and the pure pain of guaranteed heartfelt endings when the plane takes off for Calgary again. For now, welcome to this home.

Go back to that home.

Here. There. Disruptions. Intermissions. Intervals. Interludes. Pauses. Disconnections. Interruptions.

Part 2: Unexpected Intrusions

I am the interloper. I have surreptitiously arrived at the block of flats in Bedok Reservoir. I have come unannounced, quietly apprehensive all the while I was in Calgary that I might not actually make it to Singapore on this trip. Thankfully, despite delayed airplanes and airport mishaps, I am here after three long Covid years of quarantines. All these lockdown years,

I silently suffered intense foreboding, worried about my aged parents and Papa's new diagnosis of cancer.

My heartbeats intensify as I awkwardly drag my three dishevelled suitcases into the lift at the main floor deck of the familiar public Housing Development Board (HDB) high-rise building. The lift stops on the twelfth floor. I tiptoe into my family's flat. My hands tremble as I eagerly unlock the heavy lock on the front gate of the flat. No one is in the living room. Noiselessly, I leave my suitcases inside the front door. I tiptoe to the bedrooms on my left at the back of the spotless HDB flat. I see him!

Papa is slouched in his big, black, rickety armchair in his bedroom. Old. Shrivelled. Bent. How has he become 89 years old? I flinch when I see a walking stick leaning against his chair. Papa is staring at the cell phone in his hand. The grating sounds of laughter from TikTok snippets fill the air.

TikTok? My 89-year-old father is watching TikTok? When did this new activity start to happen? He holds the phone in his left palm and bites his right thumb.

Hoarsely, I whisper. "Papa. Papa."

There is no response.

I take three small steps forward and tenderly touch his left shoulder. He suddenly glances up and jumps out of his skin; his craggy, weathered face contorts in confusion. He simply cannot fathom my presence. Puzzlement flickers. Slowly and painfully, he hoists himself up from his wobbly chair, totters, and awkwardly grabs his cane. Unsteadily, he stands up. Familiar strangers. We stand face to face.

Silence.

Papa's voice quivers and inflects: "When did you arrive? How long are you here for?" Both our faces contort with unknown, unexplainable flickers of emotion. The interruption of absence builds confusing, awkward walls. I reach out my arms and put them around Papa's frail bony body. He pats my back and says, "When did your plane arrive? How long are you here for?"

I prattle on with useless information to fill the fissures of unfamiliar familiarity.

Papa nods.

It always takes time to fill these fractures of absence. There have simply been too many interruptions in our lives. I am the eternal immigrant.

Really, how long are you here for? How long am I here for? How long?

Part 3: Mummy Love

How can I count the new lines on the contour of your face
ones that have rebelliously carved themselves into your soft flesh
over the countless years I have been away
I have become a tourist in your life
a passport filled with stamps of comings and goings

Every night I lie awake in the muggy suffocating night
each window in the bedroom flung wide open
disconcertingly suspended on the twelfth floor of this HDB flat
I patiently watch the irregular shadows dance on the corner wall
distorted by the glaring night light over the sink
my eyes resentfully wide awake

The lurid lights from the streets below
cast a confusing glow deep in my psyche
my jetlagged brain unable to tell
Calgary day from Singapore night anymore

Even in the wee hours of the night
the impatient cars and buses honk and roar by
the uneven nocturnal rhythm jars my drained nerves
desperate sleep eludes me

it won't embrace my weary soul

In the mind's perplexity of new space and place
I fumble for your calloused hand
feel your feeble clasp through your unruly snores
I quietly despair in this unaccustomed bed
seeking futile uninterrupted stillness

Night sluggishly churns into daybreak
I feel your somnolent stirrings

Groggily you lean over to kiss my damp forehead
wipe away my blistering tears
you hold me close
I sink into familiar sanctuary.

Passenger

Jide Salawu

The blue flames of Pearson summer burn my throat.
The hall is filled with windrush
Of travellers clinging to their baggage.
Next in line among this swarm of passengers
At the Covid desk is me.
I lower my mask at the signal of the border guard.
Where are you from, traveller? she demands.
I drown in a debt of history,
Soyinka's telephone conversation, yellow fever,
Fela and the Kalakuta Queens,
Hoping that this time memory will wash me clean
From symptoms and shortness of breath.

The pandemic is an elegy for a world out of order.
If words can boil mouth,
I should have no tongue by now
To talk about the tales of my crossings
Makeshift boats, and children
Who die in their waters.
The earth looks too fragile to step on.
It has always been so since I left home.
Each time I worry that I have entered
The wrong dream, coughs of strangers
Take me out of yellow valleys.
I walk on towards the exit door
Into the futures in my head.

The Many Voices of You

Yejide Kilanko

Snug under the weighted blanket pulled up to her chest, Imani watched through half-closed eyes as Leonard tucked a bright blue golf shirt into a pair of brown khakis.

Probably sensing her gaze, Leonard turned in her direction. "Good morning, babe."

Imani grunted in response. Since the previous evening had ended with a heated argument over Leonard's precious heirloom, her intention was to have a minimal engagement day.

"I'm off to Fair Havens. Depending on how our golf game and conversation goes, Dad may invite the investor team over to their place for dinner," Leonard said in a measured tone.

Imani stayed silent.

Leonard sighed. "I guess I'm still in one of your anger bubbles."

No lie.

Imani pictured a watery spiked blob floating above his head. She pointed at the door. "Tardiness is beneath a Testament."

She saw frustration flash across Leonard's face. He hated it when she mimicked his father. "We'll talk about this sudden obsession with the painting when I get back."

Leonard functioned best when life went the way he planned. No interruptions. Imani turned her eyes away. There was nothing obsessive about wanting to be free in her home.

An insistent ringing sound woke Imani. She gave her cell phone a side-eye. It was too early for unwanted calls, but the sight of Journey's number brought a smile to her face. Sister friend, a force of nature, Journey featured as a main character in almost all of Imani's memories of childhood adventures.

"Hey, wanderer," Imani said.

She heard Journey suck through her teeth. "It's not my fault love kept you rooted."

Imani's lips curled into a rueful smile. After high school, she had stayed close to home while Journey left on a solo trip to South America. Journey had said that with a name like hers, it would be sacrilegious to remain rooted in the same spot. Imani was thankful when Journey moved back to Canada after the global lockdown lifted. Journey's ecstatic father built his daughter a dream home, a tiny house on their family farm in Testaville. Six months after Journey's return, they were stunned by her father's multiple sclerosis diagnosis. The constant chaperone at their high school dances, Journey's father was a lovely man.

"How's Daddy-O doing?" Imani asked.

"He's keeping his spirits up. The physio's helping."

Journey was her father's primary support, and, like Imani, an only child. "I wish I could give you a big hug."

Journey exhaled. "I'm coming to Halifax after little man arrives."

They had three more months before their world changed forever. "I'm counting down the days," Imani said.

"I bet. Exciting times. How's my Deja?"

A warm feeling washed over Imani at the sound of her daughter's name. "Your girl's still in bed."

"And the posh Mr. Testament?"

Journey had clearly expressed how she felt when Imani began dating Leonard. Even though they had all grown up in the same picturesque town on the shores of Lake Erie, Leonard was one of the Testaments of Testaville. A private boarding school kid, Leonard had not just come into the world with a silver spoon in his mouth. He had arrived with the whole flatware set. When she brought Leonard home, the consensus was that he was not one of them. Leonard's family felt the same way about Imani's farming family. It was the only thing they all agreed on.

She pursed her lips. "Out wheeling and dealing on a golf course."

"*Oho*. I know that tone. What did Leonard do?"

Imani's anger was about what he was refusing to do. "I told him how I felt about the painting."

Journey let out a shout. "Finally!"

For ten years, she'd told herself that she could live with the evidence of her people's pain hanging in what should be her safe space. It was not Leonard's fault that his great-great-grandfather had been a slave trader. But it was his fault that the tainted heirloom stayed in their home.

"*And*?" Journey asked.

Imani clicked her tongue. "He asked for more time."

"Well, it took you a decade to tell him how that damned painting made your skin crawl," Journey said. "And I'm sure Grandma Dearest has been spoon-feeding Leonard shitty hero stories about that despicable thing since he could stand in his crib."

"You're supposed to be on my side."

Journey's voice grew soft. "Girl, I'm always on your side. With just a few disclaimers."

Imani blinked back tears. "Love you."

"Love you too. I just wanted to check up on you. I've got to get Daddy up so he can take his meds. Give Deja a kiss for me."

"Will do. Call me if you need anything."

Suddenly in the mood for piping hot black tea, Imani dragged herself out of bed and headed to the kitchen. Giving up her Baileys-laced coffee was one of the few things she disliked about being pregnant.

Mug in hand, she moved through the dining room and stood in front of her low curio cabinet. The oil painting of the slave ship at the centre of her disagreement with Leonard hung above the cabinet. The full-rigged ship with tall masts commanded attention. If one didn't know the misery it had facilitated, one would be impressed by the stately façade.

Stamped on the bronze art title plate at the corner of the image were the words, THE TESTAMENT. Right below the name was the number 1800, the year her husband's great-great-grandfather, William Arthur Testament, had commissioned the painting. Slave trade was the source of the Nova Scotia Testaments' immense wealth.

Since Leonard worked for the family business, Testament Family money – sanitized through a conglomerate of legitimate companies ranging from gas stations, restaurants, newspapers, advertising companies, to other entities she didn't know– financed their life. Her life. Their well-publicized philanthropic acts sealed the respectability deal. From the day she was born, her seven-year-old Deja had had a massive trust fund. So would the much-loved child in her womb. The lump in Imani's throat grew as she rested a hand on her stomach.

Imani's eyes closed as she recalled the previous night's conversation, held exactly where she stood now.

Leonard had run nervous fingers through his lush red beard. "Imani, I can't get rid of the painting. It's a family heirloom. You know I promised my grandmother I'd keep it."

The family matriarch was back in Testaville. "I think if I called to let her know this Blackity Black granddaughter-in-law is close to setting the painting on fire, she would respond with the right degree of urgency needed to get the damned thing out of my house."

He gave her a disapproving look. "Imani, she's a ninety-five-year-old woman who is a product of her time."

Imani kissed her teeth. Leonard was always quick to run interference for his family. "Well, your grandmother doesn't live here. I do. How can this be valuable to you?"

"Honey, you're a history teacher. You know sanitizing history will lead to us forgetting the full story."

Over the past year, she had watched public monuments and memorials that for centuries had shaped public memory crack at their foundations and topple over. Something fundamental had shifted for her as she caught a glimpse of what could still be.

"Since we're preserving history. *All of it.* I hope you're ready to tell Deja how the Testaments got their money." She hated using their child as a bargaining chip, but she meant what she said.

Leonard's face turned bright red. "Deja is a child."

She held his gaze. "Children grow up. And they ask questions."

"I promise I'll do something about it," Leonard had said after some silence. "I need time."

Imani eyed the painting as she sipped on her tea. Time wasn't infinite.

"Good morning, Momma!"

Imani turned to see Deja walking towards her. Dressed in a unicorn onesie pajama, Deja had her long hair pulled into two messy red afro puffs. "Good morning, my sweetie."

"Why do you always stare at that painting?" Deja asked.

Imani sighed. She could swear that there were days when the eyes of the blurry men standing on the ship's deck followed her around the room. "It's because I don't like it."

Deja's quizzical frown was like her maternal grandmother's. "Why?"

Because once upon a time, a man, your great-great-great-grandfather, traded in human misery. Yes, he's a part of you, but you're imperfectly good.

She was going to let Leonard give the explanation. "Because I don't."

Deja's dark brown eyes blinked behind her glasses. "Since Nanny likes the painting, maybe she should take it to her house?"

Imani reached out and stroked their daughter's cheek. Getting the painting out of her sight wouldn't get it out of her mind. But it would allow her to breathe in relative peace while she contemplated whether her simmering resentment towards Leonard was a phase or something they needed to air out.

"That is a good idea. I'll tell Daddy when he gets home." Imani held out her hand. "It's hair wash day. We should eat some breakfast before we get started."

Deja grabbed her hand. "Blueberry pancakes, please."

They headed for the kitchen. Long-limbed like her father, Deja had also inherited the cheeky grin that had held Imani's attention all those years ago. "Your godmother called while you were asleep. She said to give you a kiss."

Deja smiled. Journey, who never forgot to call on Deja's birthdays, was one of her daughter's favourite people. "You talk and laugh differently with Auntie Journey," Deja said.

Imani paused. This was news to her. "I do?"

"You sound like you're singing a happy song." Deja scrunched her nose. "And when talking to Nanny and Papa, you sound like this. *Deja honey, please use your indoor voice. We don't speak this way.*"

Imani's jaw dropped. "I don't talk like that."

"Yes, you do, Momma. Your voice is high like Nanny's. *Imani, surely your husband mentioned that we would be visiting.*"

Leonard usually made the announcement minutes before their arrival. His deliberate act ensured Imani had less time to escape. To be fair to them, despite their subtle, apologetic behaviour it was she who had chosen to maintain the distance their initial disapproval of her had created. Limited interaction minimized the chance for additional hurt feelings. "I do not sound like that."

Deja gave her a solemn look. "You do."

She couldn't win the argument. "Do I have a different voice when talking to you?"

Deja nodded. "Low and soft. Like when you're talking to a baby." Deja lifted her chin. "I know when it's a telemarketer calling too."

Imani chuckled. "That's because you're my smart baby."

"I am not a baby," Deja said with the righteous indignation of a grown seven-year-old.

She gazed at her daughter's face. *What do I sound like when I'm with Daddy?* The question lodged at the back of Imani's throat.

"Momma?"

"Yes, sweetie."

Deja cocked her head. "One day, am I going to have many voices like you?"

She tightened the hold on Deja's hand. "No, my love. You're going to have one strong voice."

Imani had read somewhere that dark chocolate works wonders for a depleted heart. She unwrapped a bar of Godiva, broke off a piece, and popped it into her mouth. With Deja asleep and Leonard still with his parents, she could test the hypothesis all evening.

As Leonard walked into their bedroom, she gave the third chocolate bar a contemplative look. Even though he disliked it, he didn't comment on her eating in bed.

"The meeting went well," Leonard said as he sat beside her. "It's up to the lawyers now."

Silent, Imani focused on the sweetness in her mouth as Leonard moved closer to her. His intentions were clear. Regardless of what was going on in their world, the chemistry between them remained intact. Their lovemaking ranged across a spectrum from quick and intense to sensual unravelling. But no matter how deep they dove into each other, they still had to come up for air.

Ignoring her stillness, Leonard began nibbling on her earlobe. The man knew her weak points. The gentle hand placed on his arm told him no.

Leonard groaned as he moved away. "Imani, what do you want from me?"

The fear was that what she wanted from Leonard, he couldn't give. Imani ran a shaky hand over her face. For far too long, she had told herself that no one walks through every space as their authentic self, that everyone shapeshifts to survive. *Right?*

She knew she could simply have the painting bubble-wrapped and delivered to his office, but she needed Leonard to be the one to put it out of the house. It would say to her, Imani, I choose you. Yes, Leonard had married her against his parent's wishes. Given their hold on him, that was a big deal. But she needed him to keep choosing her for a lifetime.

"I feel like you're punishing me for something I didn't do," Leonard said.

"I can understand why that must suck for you."

Leonard sighed. "Yet, the look on your face says you don't give a flying fig."

He knew her preferred word. And right now, she didn't give two of them. The conversation with Deja came back to her mind. "Leonard, how many voices do I have?"

The quick laugh on Leonard's lips died as she continued to stare at him. "Voices?"

"Yes."

"One. Hopefully."

Imani sighed. "Perhaps I would feel better if you acknowledged that you still benefit from it?"

They both knew what *it* referred to.

For a moment, Leonard hung his head. When he looked up at her, she saw a troubled man. "Oh, I acknowledge *it*. I don't talk about *it* because a part of me says, whoopee-doo, then what?" He wove his hand around. "Walk away from the only life I've had? I don't know if I can live that way."

Something clicked in her head as she stared at Leonard's wan face. She couldn't spend the rest of her life captive to these feelings of displacement. Leonard had his faults. But he wasn't responsible for fixing what she had allowed to become fragmented.

"I'm going home," she said.

Leonard frowned. "Imani, this is your home."

"I meant Testaville. It's been a while since I visited."

"But your parents are in Florida," he said.

Her parents were now dedicated snowbirds. "I'll stay with Journey. It will be good to also spend some time with her dad."

Leonard opened and closed his mouth before reaching for her hand. "Is it safe for you to travel?"

"It is."

He gave her a pleading look. "Can I come with you?"

Imani shook her head. This was something she had to do alone.

Leonard's voice had a slight tremble. "You're taking Deja with you?"

She knew the real question Leonard wanted to ask her was, *Are you coming back?*

Their paths had first crossed at their local ice cream shop. It took a year before she agreed to date Leonard. It was hard for her to decide to become a constant in someone else's life when she was still learning how to fully show up in her own. Because Leonard was so sure of who he was, she had hoped that his shiny confidence would be enough to carry them both. Not forever. But enough until she was ready. For Deja, the child inside her and herself, she had to become prepared.

She gave his hand a gentle squeeze. "No. I'll be gone for two weeks at the most."

Leonard looked like he was about to cry. "I love you, Imani Ashe."

Imani swallowed the lump in her throat. She loved him still. "I know."

My Canadian Student Visa Experience and an Interrupting Bureaucracy

Ademola Adesola

What I share and reflect on in this piece is the story of my journey from Nigeria, West Africa, to Canada for a doctoral research program. There is a story behind every completed doctoral project. Here is an aspect of mine. I applied four times for a Canadian student visa; I was unjustifiably refused three times.

Although I eventually made it to the University of Manitoba (U of M) and completed my PhD research in record time, I had to scale several interrupting hurdles. Frankly, I almost did not make it to the U of M. Was my plan for that degree interrupted because securing admission was taxing? No. Were the numerous interruptions I encountered because of financial constraints? Far from it. Were unforeseen family matters responsible for the darts of interruptions I had to fend off? Nope. Just what was responsible for the steep mountains of interruptions that I had to, like Sisyphus, repeatedly climb to travel to Canada? It was the bureaucratic behemoth known as Immigration, Refugees and Citizenship Canada, aka the IRCC. Dealing with that entity caused inexplicable breaks in the continuity and fruition of an immigration plan.

To encounter the IRCC as a Black/African person seeking to migrate to Canada is to open a history book of stories of many African/Black folks who suffered baffling interruptions on account of the historical immigration policy that banned "any immigrants belonging to the Negro race," as stated in a 1911 federal Order-in-Council issued during Prime Minister Sir Wilfrid Laurier's administration.

My application to the U of M Faculty of Graduate Studies for an admission to the PhD program in the Department of English, Theatre, Film, and Media was, from the beginning to the end, smooth and sweet.

After a consultation with a doctoral student in the same university and department, I chose the U of M as the ideal place for me to undertake my doctoral research.

It was clear to me that I had to exit Nigeria and go elsewhere to give more meaning to my life. I was ready to discontinue my PhD work at the university in Nigeria from which I had received two other degrees. I was no stranger to the dysfunction crippling the critical sectors of Nigeria. I had worked in that country as a journalist, a senior political assistant, and a university lecturer. At that point, I was convinced that the backward governance logic that supervened across my country of birth was deeply entrenched and that change would take decades to happen. I love the country; my displeasure is with the worst people who successively have run it in different administrative layers.

Canada would be my destination. And so, to the U of M Faculty of Graduate Studies (FGS) I applied. A few months later, close to bedtime in Nigeria, I received a letter informing me of the success of my application. I recall the pure joy inspired by that communication. My partner Tolu and I were beside ourselves with joy and could not sleep. Far into the night we talked about the program. We conversed about the sacrifices to be made individually and collectively. We met minds on the interruption we must endure. Our son was barely two years old. Tolu and I imagined the pain and confusion the boy would deal with on account of my temporary physical absence from his life. In the wee hours of the following morning, we eventually succumbed to the power of sleep. At least the interrupter of our sleep was a joyous development. But a different and vicious interrupter took charge weeks after that night.

Once the excitement of the admission had run its full course, Tolu and I transited into the second phase of action: student visa application. We read the available information on the IRCC portal. My Nigerian acquaintance at the U of M had gone through the IRCC corridor of discomfort and delay. The slap on the wrist he had gotten from the IRCC was a wacky delay. We mined him for information on the application process. Tolu and I worked diligently to meet the conditions the IRCC outlined for the required visa category. With all boxes checked, I sent in my application to the IRCC for a student visa in March 2015. Between April and August, when I planned to travel to Canada for the start of my studies in September, there was enough time. But I did not know that the ample time would mean nothing for my plans.

In May of that year, I received a response to my student visa application from the IRCC. As I threaded through my account to access the main communication, I could feel palpitations of happiness rising in my being. The courteous opening statement of the IRCC letter belied its plan-interrupting decision. In seconds, once faced with the rejection, I experienced a mélange of disbelief, disappointment, discomfort. According to the letter, the officer who had processed my application was not convinced that I had enough money to coordinate my affairs in Canada. Other woolly reasons were given.

This was my first application to the IRCC. It would take a year or two for me to adopt the view that the IRCC is adept at pulling a rabbit out of the hat to justify its rejection of visa applications from my side of the world. Had the IRCC not rejected a Kenyan's visitor visa application on the strange ground that the applicant had only travelled within the African continent?

I rationalized my first rejection for a student visa as a mistake. Without hanging fire, Tolu and I decided that we still had time to put in another application. We thought of an appeal, but were counselled against it. In fact, we found the closing statement beneath the outlined reasons for rejection encouraging. That statement urged a new application, provided the reasons for the failure of the initial application could be taken care of. It also asked for a new application fee. The tone of that communication was unmistakably one of *you must begin again*.

We began again. I sent in another application. I went above and beyond to prove anew that I would not leech off the Canadian state while studying. I had some funding for my program of studies and would bring more money with me. I provided other relevant documents. But before September 2015 I received a decision communication to my second application, a boilerplate refusal. Perhaps the only new item was the statement that I did not have strong ties in my country of birth.

I was in my early thirties and had not spent more than a week anywhere outside Nigeria prior to that time. My nucleus and extended family were based in Nigeria. My work life and crusade (through appearances on radio and TV stations and newspaper articles) for a Nigeria ordered by sense, ideas, and visions were deeply rooted into the soil of that misgoverned space. Tolu and I also had land assets and went about our daily affairs using our family car. There were more things that connected me to that country. Yet, according to an IRCC officer, who had rummaged through a sheaf of application forms detailing some aspects of my life, I had no ties to and in Nigeria.

In my view, that misplaced conclusion was another form of erasure of the Black person. I felt that the organization seemed to encourage applicants such as me to be something else or rework themselves before they can be considered worthy of visa.

With the second rejection of my student visa application, it became apparent to me that my plan to begin my studies that year had been interrupted. Thus began the first of three deferments of my research program. I deferred my admission, deciding to apply again the following year for a visa. The third application happened early the following year. Again, I put the application together after I had studiously reviewed the grounds for rejection of the previous two applications. In fact, following the recommendation of an elderly acquaintance, I paid an immigration consultant to investigate the IRCC decision on my application by requesting the full document. There was nothing of significance in the result, which repeated the same unfounded reasons officially made available to me.

My third application would be more useful in my coming to terms with what I consider to be IRCC discrimination against Black/African visa applicants. Whatever improvement I made to that application did not cut any ice with the IRCC.

This application was unique compared to the previous two. One, the IRCC response time was longer. Two, in Hamlet's words, the immigration establishment spoke daggers to me without using any. At some point in the process, the IRCC asked me to go for my medical. From the cases I was privy to, I gathered that once an applicant received that request, the probability that the application would sail through was 9.9/10. I got the medical done. About five weeks later, the IRCC informed me that I had passed the medical. I began to set plans in motion for my travel, believing that that third application would be positively processed. In fact, while waiting my turn to see a doctor for the medical exam, the Muse came visiting and I wrote a longish satiric prose poem of gratitude to my land of birth ("Gratitude to the Land of My Birth"), informing it of my imminent departure from its *livable* borders.

I was wrong. Or had the Muse spoken to me as the witches had spoken to Macbeth? When the decision information from the IRCC came, it said what the previous two had etched indelibly on my mind.

After my third try for a student visa hit the rock of refusal, I wrote to the then Graduate Chair of my department informing him of my disinterest in the program on account of visa palaver. He was so sorry to read my decision. As regards immigration matters, I feel that Canadian post-secondary institutions are lame ducks. I still wonder what those letters from Graduate Chairs meant in the application process for a student visa. But the Chair did not think that the third rejection should sound the death knell for my quest to come to the department for my research.

About two days later, he wrote me again asking if I would like to defer my program for a third time. In his view, another attempt for a study visa could succeed. He had witnessed it happen before. I thought he was playing a cruel game with my head. Was I a glutton for rejection by the IRCC? What could a fourth application for the same visa possibly do that the previous three attempts got wrong? I would rather go on with my PhD project at Obafemi Awolowo University, Nigeria, where I had gotten my two degrees. However, a few days later I gave thought again to the chair's advice. The sane demon in my mind called me to a tête-à-tête and asked me one vital question: "What would you lose if you put in a third letter of deferment for your program at U of M? Didn't the Chair say the department would seek approval for it at the Faculty of Graduate Studies?" I gave in and put in my third deferment letter. Thus began my fourth attempt at a student visa to study in Canada.

After my fourth application, I was left in a terrifying wilderness of waiting. The wait was long. By September 2017, the start of the fall term, when I was to begin my doctoral studies, the IRCC had not said anything to me about my fourth application. One month into the semester, it was still quiet. Meanwhile, the demons of taunt and mockery were actively at work in my head, having a good time at the expense of my sanity.

In October, the IRCC wrote to me asking me to inquire from my department if I could still join classes for the term or get a new admission letter to begin my studies the following semester. It was futile to start classes in a North American university four weeks into the term. Starting classes in a North American institution one month into the semester would be the easiest pathway to poor performance for anyone coming from a largely different educational system. Without hanging fire, my Department and I agreed to ask the Faculty of Graduate Studies for a new admission letter. That was easy. After all, the faculty had at that time become used to issuing new admission letters to me.

In November 2017, the IRCC— interrupter of my postgraduate studies plan—approved my fourth application for a study permit. What had I done differently this fourth time? This is perhaps a relevant research question for anyone interested in conducting a doctoral study in immigration matters, especially the Canadian variant. I wonder if my being from one of the "dirty 30" countries that the IRCC has put a big question mark on had any role to play in the rejections of my three consecutive applications for a student visa.

In December 2017, I left Nigeria for Canada for my PhD. Tolu and I had planned that after two years into my study, she, our son, and the second child we were expecting would join me in Canada. But the IRCC denied our first application. It poisoned and protracted a positively designed brief familial separation. We put in a second application after some months. That second try would succeed. Again, we had done nothing radically different from the first application.

I reunited with my family and began the work of bonding, especially with the youngest member, who was just a year old at the time (one who forced a poem from me during my waiting period for the approval of the family visa application. The poem is titled "ADUNNI: One Who's Sweet to Have." Adunni is the name she got from me at birth in my physical absence).

I targeted completing my doctoral program in four years. My immigration experience was one reason for that decision. Another reason was that I was convinced it was possible to finish the program in four years, having seen some people do so without sacrificing quality and excellence. Besides, considering my experience with the unfathomable IRCC, I did not want to take liberties with time regarding my studies.

Did the IRCC interrupt my flow of life again a few years after my family joined me in Canada? Yes. No matter how torrential the rain, it cannot wash off the spots on a leopard's skin. Four months before the expiration of our temporary resident permits, we applied for a renewal. At that point, Tolu was the principal applicant. We paid all the application fees for the entire four family members. And we waited. When the IRCC responded a few months later, it was a rude awakening. The IRCC had approved the renewal request of three members of the family but rejected one. The rejected request was Tolu's. Why? The IRCC said she had not paid the required application fee. To avoid further delays we decided to send in a new application with the full complement of another application charge.

The following day we contacted the IRCC and presented its error to it. After some repeated returns to a supervisor, the agent who attended to us confirmed the receipt of the application fee that they claimed we had not paid. Then we thought there would be a reversal of the error. Far from it. The IRCC asked us to apply again. "But do not pay another application fee," the agent instructed. We wrote a letter thereafter to the IRCC about that injustice. The main response we received taught us to see Canada in one of the couplets in Maya Angelou's poem, "America" – "Her borders of justice/not clearly defined." We got our money back after the new application was approved, an approval that sentenced us to another mind-wracking waiting. This time around, COVID-19 was a good excuse, but the IRCC forgot that all that the pestilence did was to worsen an already bad processing situation. Among the three renewed permits the IRCC should have sent to us, only one arrived. All explanations to them that the other two must have been lost somewhere fell on ears unamenable to our voices.

We were *ordered* to wait another six weeks for the approved documents to arrive. While waiting, we lost many things, including our medical coverage.

In my opinion, the IRCC is a broken bureaucracy. Unless it genuinely accepts that it needs a revolutionary overhaul, it will continue to interrupt and do real damage to student applicants' educational plans and family reunification schemes, and distress many more applicants who need work permits, permanent residency, etc. I think the IRCC would also need to do away with the idea that it is doing visa applicants a favour or that getting whatever visa to Canada is a privilege. How so? Those applicants spend a lot on their bid to get approval to come to Canada and to renew their residency permits within it. Applicants for student visas from my country of birth and other African countries meet the requirements for that category of visa, despite the unfairness in those requirements. The notion that we can try another country if we do not appreciate how the IRCC operates signposts an unwillingness to reflect on and review how the establishment functions. Most Black/African immigrants in Canada add value to the country in many meaningful ways. We are happy to live and work here. The process of being here should not be rigged against us, especially Africans. As someone who has experienced the IRCC's interruptions to what should be a thing of happiness, I hope to continue to work with others genuinely interested in advocating for a just, efficient IRCC.

Interrupted Sepia

Clara A.B. Joseph

An undulating tongue, some white skin,
traces of the meeting.
Has anyone written a more vivid history, fought
fewer masters in the factories
where we prayed? You and I

and our dreams of love arrived.
I was proud of your words,
muffled by lip and touch.
The hut of our vows was perfect;
the breeze was gentle, like the beloved's tickle,
all set to continue for centuries. Curls of kitchen smoke
filled my vision. All that became as if

things of the past
in brittle sepia pages
with well-drawn margins. Then, History began
to shout: "Why baptize the baptized!
Why bead the black
peppercorn rosary! Why swap the script!
Whitewashed, St. Thomas of India has lost
his right to doubt. The visitors have gone
back, and the Discourse
thrives again on this land. Each morn
is calved, the hour is milched, and the day is never
slaughtered. How nice this is in a dream."
In the marketplace was badness.

A reverie settled itself as far
as the seraphic skyline. And if I felt
something, if I put a tiny me in this
space, announced for once
my hurt? I shall bleed
onto these pages.
A benign ghost of premonition rested on my keyboard
one day, but we had all been taught
to ignore the netherworld. Life marches;
it gets proper.

MINDWALKS

Intrusion

Samantha Jones

This is a morning routine
This is a house
This is a kitchen
This is a large appliance
Check the stovetop
This is a small appliance
Check the coffeemaker
This is a small appliance
Check the toaster
This is a door
Locked locked locked locked
This is a person leaving their house
Locked locked locked locked
This is a person leaving their house
Locked locked locked locked
This is a person leaving their house
Locked locked locked locked
This is a person leaving their house
This is a pause this is a pause on the stairs this is a pause
This is a pause on the stairs this is a pause
This is a person leaving their house

The house the house the house the house

The locks the doors the kitchen the plugs

Return to the house
Return to the house
Return to the house
Return to the house

This is a person away from their house
This is a Möbius strip

This is a typical day
This is a day at the office *Return to the house*
This is an expectation *Return to the house*
This is a mouse click this is a moRsetuolicko *the house*
This is a list *Return to the house*
This is a hand writing a list *Return to the house*
This is a due date *Return to the house*
This is a responsibility *Don't make a mistake*
This is a collaboration *Don't make a mistake it will*
impact other people
This is a collaDoratiomakDon'trnistakeaitmisltakeiptactilother
jrepplet other people
Dhis'tsmadellabroisatiken
*Dhis'tsmadellabroisattke*waiting
Dhis'tsmakitingnistake
Dhis'tsmakitingnistake

This is an evening routine
This is a restful sleep *These are all of the things you should*
This is a restful sleep *have done today*
This is a restful Sleep *These are all of the things you need to*
This is a restful sleep *do tomorrow*
This is the clock at 3:00 am *These are all of the things you have been*
procrastinating This is sitting *interrupted*
This is a list this is a list this is a list this is a list this is a list this is a list this is this this

This is distress
This is a pillow *to summons*
This will pass *This is a pillow shifted*
This will pass *The covers uncovered covered uncovered covered*
This will pass
This will pass
This is the mistake *Summon the breath*
This is the breath *Summon the incomplete*
This is *Summon the breath*
This *Summon the breath*

This is a Möbius strip

this is a pillow

Tai Chi Mind Games

Gina Roitman

1. The Prep

The intention is clear. Head to the basement. Turn on Kitajima's meditation CD "The Source." Take up the stance and prepare for fifteen minutes of Tai Chi Chu'an.

I love my daily Tai Chi routine, a moving meditation. It is possible that my whole life is a moving meditation, the healthy repetition of daily cycles punctuated by unplanned, sometimes unpleasant, interruptions.

What appeals most is that Tai Chi has the power to stretch every muscle in my body while my brain wanders off, lost in memories or unexplored territory. As with life, I move through Tai Chi without a plan, allowing each move, each turn—quarter, half, or full—to lead me to the next step, the next place to put my foot down just so. I work at being careful, to keep in balance.

Since I first took it up more than twenty years ago, Tai Chi has become an essential part of my well-being. Despite countless efforts, I proved hopeless at traditional meditation, no matter how hard I worked at not making a conscious effort to empty my mind. I tried sitting still to allow my mind to be silent, but the effort invariably resulted in an unplanned snooze. I am renowned as an excellent snoozer, but otherwise, not so good at remaining still. I also need Tai Chi because I have a little ADHD.

I learned the 108-movement Wu discipline from Tai Chi Tom, a successful aerospace engineer who generously shared the knowledge he had acquired in China as a teenager. My ex, Gary, introduced me to

Tom, but then, in his usual fashion, Gary lost interest in the process. Too much work, he said.

When young, Tom had contracted a fatal illness for which doctors in Canada claimed there was no cure. As a last resort, his parents sent him to China, where part of his treatment included the practice of Tai Chi Chu'an. Tom never revealed which illness nearly killed him, but when he didn't die, he returned to Montreal and out of gratitude, decided to share his knowledge of the martial art.

Tom was a born teacher.

'Let your body learn the motions,' he would softly intone during our Wednesday night sessions. He held these in the lunchroom of his aerospace engineering plant in Lachine, where the odour of iron filings, Chinese spices, and deli meats had a surprisingly comforting effect.

'Do it without any thought of controlling your progress,' he emphasized. Over the years, friends have asked me to teach them the movements, but as soon as I start to describe the simultaneous position of hands, feet, arms, and legs, all moving in tandem, I get buggered up. Thinking about which movement will come next ensures that I immediately lose my place. For me, the different positions through which I glide are like snapshots in my mind. I can usually tell when I have screwed up if I find myself facing in the wrong direction. I hate losing my place and having to start over. Losing your place is not uncommon for those of us who live with attention-deficit.

2. The Process

I begin.

I plant my feet slightly apart, face the window and prepare for the salutation to the earth. (*I really should know the names of more of these moves, but Tom never said anything except 'Follow me.'*)

Legs apart, knees slightly bent, hands float up from the floor, palms down. Crouch, rise, raise arms, quarter turn, move palms into a T. Push.

Quarter turn to the right, hands face inward, and with the sweep of one arm and then the next, pivot and push the palm away from the body three times in a 'graceful balletic' motion. (*That's what Adele once called it when I was showing off my moves one Sunday. It is probably the nicest thing she ever said to me. She and I were sisters-in-law trapped in a Sunday-with-the-family loop...every Sunday for brunch at the home of Gary's brother ... every Sunday! Same menu, same conversations...sometimes I felt so trapped I considered gnawing off my own leg. When I heard Adele call me graceful, I was dumbfounded as I was the tallest female in the family, and felt like a moose among the mice.)*

Quarter turn left, begin to sweep arms right, left. Repeat three times. (*The plant on the windowsill needs watering.)* Lift hands towards face in a motion like splashing water, then bend backwards. (*When I was a kid, I could go all the way down. Charged kids a nickel to watch me. Gawd! The disappointment when I didn't split my head open on the sidewalk...a long time ago.*) Take three steps back, sweep arms, twist core. (*I love the pleasant sound of my neck cracking. I sure could use a massage, though. Vicky is no longer an option. She talks too much instead of working out the knot in my shoulders. I wonder if there is someone else nearby...I should do a Google search*). Cross legs into open scissors, arms out for balance, drop down into a squat, rise in one smooth motion. (*My favourite move. Boy! I remember the look on Eli's face when we compared notes about similarities in Tai Chi and karate. He didn't see that one coming. He was... what? Seven at the time and now he's getting ready for his bar mitzvah. I'd better start saving for that.)* Pause. (*Where was I? Orient yourself.)* Repeat the arm sweeps with accompanying palm twists, push arms away from the body, fend off a possible attack, draw the palms back to gather in strength. (*Tom emphasized that Tai Chi was a martial art intended to defend personal space, not to strike. I guess by leaving Gary I defended my future space from a dead-end marriage. I went as far as I could go, moving to Europe. Those six months in France, especially Sundays, were heaven...a lifetime ago.)* Quarter turn, lift right leg. Bend. Place foot next to inside of left knee, arms out. Kick leg free like a crane ready for takeoff. (*That was when I had my first go-around with Axel, who swooped into my life at just the right moment. But life has always been full of twists and turns. Takeoffs and landings. He took off after a while, but I landed on my feet.*) Repeat. Left foot against right knee, lift leg up, kick out. Balance on right foot. (*Feels good, but wait...did I skip a sequence?)* Stop. *(No, I'm good…)* Move forward two paces and slide the arm through the hand with a closed fist. Rotate hands in defense, cross ankles, turn 360 degrees. (*Oops. Took the turn too fast…it's the way I always go at life. Have to slow down. Remember, I'm not seventy anymore.)*

Reposition. Raise hands in defense. Flutter from the wrist—once, twice. Circle arms wide *(Like cleaning the bathroom mirror while wondering whose face is that anyway?)* once to the right. Pivot. Do it again, once to the left. *(I often thought that this movement would lure Axel back…if I just kept doing it. Then, after a few years, I stopped thinking about him...)*

Repeat. Quarter turn left, begin to sweep arms right, then left. Repeat three times. (*I was determined not to make the mistakes of my youth. If he wanted me, loved me, I figured he'd come and get me.)* Take two steps back, sweep arms, twist core. Repeat leg cross, scissor, arms out for balance, drop into a squat. Rise. Pull back. Lift left leg. Right hand taps left ankle. *(I'm on a roll this morning. Should do the whole routine over again or maybe lift some weights…keep my arms trim.* Lift leg, broken wing like a wounded crane…turn and…

"Gina, à table!" Axel calls down from the kitchen. "Breakfast is ready."

I stop. "Just a minute."

(Damn…where was I? Think…don't think…never mind.)

"Okay. I'm coming, Sweetie."

(*Repeat again tomorrow.)*

Duri

Gian Marco Visconti

Duri is the word,
distesa sopra l'atmosfera

a desolate ceiling
stretched over the earth's shell,
an open sea of its own kind

we are the contents that fill the void:
without us there is no distance to count
no sense of lasting, nor ending

*

piccoli scogli più
piccolissimi spazi tra di loro

the path is littered
with caltrops
they're just tiny rocks
with even tinier gaps
between them

la distanza dall'uno ad altro

è (in)finita nella sua sciagura
nella sua durezza

collisions at a distance
(in)finite in their misfortune
in their duress

duri comes into my home
and spills itself over the hardwood

mara Maula tame dur nathi
maru dukh dur karo

must i translate for you reader
my most sacred thoughts?

is this space between us
one that must be closed?

how can I keep
il nullo qua dentro

i will not explain this
if you do not speak
the language of rupture

my mother tongues are already broken
enough

*

the sparrows are the same everywhere
but a better sight when my love is near

accanto a me, he flutters from word to word,
whittling the dread down to polvere

a silent engraving appears upon me:
ovunque tu sia, c'è il sole durevole

i concede:
wherever you are, there is endless sunlight

i remain, flightless in your glare.

Trellis

Alison Clarke

Mortar of metal and sand, stardust and pixie dust, sauntering through the air…

I should be

I Should Be

Interrupter

I was waltzing, walking in starlight, iridescent,

dreamscape, DreamDance

Interrupter

I should be   cleaning   dusting   organizing

Housework   yardwork   cleaning out leaves from the gutter

I n t e r

I   n   t   e   r

I   Should

I   should

I

S   h   o   u   l   d

I –

I

I

A unicorn gleams bronze, a firefly glows in the dark, the …

Blue Ridge Mountains are calling

A dragon draws her first breath,

A faerie smiles and knows

She will be her best friend, They will sit, They will sit,

ON A

Trellis

OF STARS

I N T E R

I N T E R

The Sisters Of Light,

Love, They smile, They laugh,
They dance

The girls hug each other, and embrace:
A sanscript of sea and sound
Angels upon high, they glitter and glow resplendent
in their robes

I should be working on a project, an assignment,
University, Uni,
I should be

Deadlines

D E A D L I N E S

I n t e r r u p t e r

I n t e r r u p t e r

I N T E R –

I N T E R

I N

I N

I N

Little Love Songs

Anna Marie Sewell

Più Vivo: In Moonlight

Joe was the one who had the most fun — wherever they went, whenever they played, he was wild and crazy and surging with joy.

Underneath it was a boy afraid he wasn't good enough, but the world wasn't supposed to see that. Inevitably, women did see it and eagerly reached out to him, both for the fun and with tenderness for the little boy. And he let them in and played with them, too. But none of them got to touch the little boy heart of him. Until Linda.

She came up to him after yet another show, and walked beside him, asking about his guitar, could he show her a few things. He thought about the things he liked to show girls, and said sure, sure, but then he gave her more than a casual sideways glance, and slowed his steps.

She was so young. Not necessarily in years— he didn't care too much one way or another about that, and never worried, because it was the older chicks who liked him, so he assumed she was old enough. But she was looking at him frankly, without sex, just longing to get into the music.

It was too late, she was with him now, but he thought fast, and said, *look, I have to meet with a woman. She is not going to be happy to make a good deal with me if you are with me, so I'll come back to you. Where is your car?* He steered her toward her little blue car, and he put his guitar case in the back seat.

I'll be back, okay? The guitar sat there like a talisman, and so she told him where to find her.

And off he went, and the woman was there, like every other woman, offering what he wanted but also sex, and he found himself saying, *I will come back, I want the deal, but I have to go pick up Linda.*

The woman looked puzzled— was this kinky?

He ran out the door, ran pell-mell back to Linda and said with his hands pressed to his knees, back heaving for breath, *come with me.*

He took her hand. He swept her into his arms. She whispered something with her face pressed to his chest, and he simply murmured *mm mm mm* in response.

Come with me. And can you drive?

And she did, and he sat beside her. And said, improbably, *you look like an elf.*

And he took her hand and led her into the woman's place, and said, *this is my Linda.* And the woman, being a sport, did not complain. But she could see that this woman meant something to him that she'd never seen before. And he sat Linda on the sofa, and sat beside her, chuckling self-consciously, and pulled a ratty afghan around her and kissed her helplessly.

The thing is, he said unprompted, *I thought this girl was just another girl. But then I learned we are elves in the moonlight.* He laughed again, a strange sound that sounded as if it startled him as much as anyone.

The woman gave Joe his package deal, signed and solid, and said, *go, go now, softly,*

and they left, and his arm was around Linda's waist, and she walked as if startled, too. She'd never expected this.

And they walked, close together, through the night, and he smiled and laughed and stopped from time to time to kiss her, drinking moonlight from her skin.

When morning came, they were curled together on a park bench. His eyes were dark as thunder with desire and fear, and she knew he was going to run.

And he ran.

And she smiled all through the next time, and hung little ornaments around the park, telling herself and the birds, *yes, it's true. I belonged with him, that rock star.*

And she didn't know if he'd come back, but she knew that night was true and real. And she hung small ornaments as testimony that she would always remain a little bit in that night, his one rock of certainty in the crazy world he rolled through.

When he sobered up, she was high in his mind and heart, but she was the one thing he didn't speak of in rehab, just as he'd never spoken of her to the band.

The birds found her body in the park before the humans did and lifted away; her hair and her faded blue shawl, thread by thread, something like silver trailing after them as they flew.

Più Lento: Snow Fall

He was nice. Not like the other boys. Gentle, you might say. His dark curly hair hung in a bit of a mop, his long face was serious yet cat-like, and he didn't have that sort of crazy energy, that 'laddish' thing.

He was just nice. Easy to be around. Interested and observant. The other kids—we were all just kids, really, playing at being grown-up—were obsessed with their love triangulations, and who was going to end up with that young man whose name I don't even recall now. I remember he liked that all the girls looked at him that way, and that he could have his pick. I had been his first choice, before we knew what he was like, and so all that made me was the first to be thrown over.

Marce and Nancy were at that time fighting over his affections, so I went with Michael, to show him how to get to the music shop in the old town. We went on the train, remarking about the differences between European trains, built into pre-existing street patterns built for people and horses to traverse, and Calgarian trains, built into the boulevards of sprawl.

We got on the train back uptown, talking about how everyone else was ranting about the elections, how tired and useless that talk is. He said we could not live by repeating talking points, we had to focus on action and innovation. On making things. Making harmonies. Making new songs that people would love and honouring the best of the masters' songs. And in his eyes, I saw the world a better place, a place where Michael's long black coat, his scarf, his laughter over the curve of a letter on a sign in the distance as the train glided by, and his music— especially his music— would all be welcomed.

I wanted to be in that place.

And then the train eased 'round into our street, and stopped, and people jumped out. And Michael jumped out, into the snow. *No, Michael,* I scolded, laughing. I knew I could jump, too, and then we could walk from there, but we'd be late and covered in snow. And I knew it didn't matter to me if we were late, and that the only reason I urged him to get back on the train was to protect him from the rest of them. I didn't want them talking about us. So, maybe I was protecting me, too. I just didn't want this moment between us to be labelled.

Anyway, he laughed back at me, inside the train, and he threw his flute case, perfectly, elegantly, up to me. I caught it, noticing how perfectly it described him, for it was effortlessly, naturally beautiful. It was scuffed and dull, a case that had been put to good use, carried through many adventures, undimmed for all that it was simply not a thing he cared to polish or show off. It was confident, that case, because it was doing what it was made for.

I swung it in one hand lightly and contemplated jumping out now. Surely the doors were about to close, and it was almost too late.

Michael! I shouted.

Arriba! he replied, joyfully, and grabbed the pole in the doorway, and swung one foot up, like a pirate.

Hurry! I said, still laughing, but afraid in the pit of my stomach, all this in a flash, because time had made space for all this to happen before the train doors would close. The train began to move, and the door sensor must have known his hand meant a person, so the door stayed open, and he hopped on his grounded foot, and made to swing himself entirely after his foot and hand. But it was all snowy out there, and he slipped, and his hand and foot could not hold him in safety, on the train. They could only keep him close enough for the momentum to swing him under.

Of course, the train stopped immediately when it hit him. There are safety measures. But I crouched there, with his grey flute case in my hand, just staring at the empty whiteness outside. And I knew that time would not be merciful and speed back up, nor would it change course, go back, go sideways, do anything to get us to a place where I would not have to drop out of the still-open door, and run to him, the tiny horrendous distance to where he lay in the snow.

Michael! I cried, unable to look either at him or away. How had I never grasped his magnificence, his luminous grace? I caught the shabby flute case. I'd never dared to take his hand. I could not do so now.

Why?

Snow kissed him. Earth held him. He stilled. The air stank of metal, and his words hung like stars of frost.

I don't know.

BODY CHECKS

A Song for the Body and What it Can Bear

Jenna Butler

I.

The weight of the rain that does not come calling. The fleet of bright feeders bereft of all birds. The new dryland garden so long in its growing. The cistern gone, fulsome and claggy with weed.

The goldfinches doled out like high-summer pennies. The arcs of the cranes passing over for days. The deep, tender space in the bowl of the breast. The rootlet of fear worried at like a tooth.

The orchard grown lush despite stuttering seasons. The wheatfields all slattern with thistles and grass. The body that falters in August's long furnace. The shadows of rainclouds that gather and pass.

The deep, tender space in the bowl of the breast.
The rootlet of fear worried at like a tooth.
The hope that abides between grieving and anger.
The certain old sun and the balm of the moon.

II.

There were things that we knew. A good berrying season meant a hard winter. Wasps' nests high in the underbrush signalled deep snow coming.

There were things that we knew; now we're lost in altered patterns. A thick fleece of clouds drives the honeybees home, but the rain that threatens never comes. Out go the bees again. Everybody is dry and terse, a little irate, those with stingers and those without.

We lean into the spaces where knowledge used to be. The beaked willows flower a full week earlier, but the wild bees break their hibernation at the same time they have always done. We plant pussy willows to flourish in the gap, rich catkins a kind of bridge.

Working with the land has always been a manifestation of hope. Even in hard years, seasons lost to drought or flood, the dream is of *enough*—to feed a family, a community. Even as the climate changes, weather mercurial and dry, we sow, we preserve, we pass forward what we have saved.

Lilac time meant planting out tomatoes. Now the frost comes late, unpredictable. We move the tomatoes under cover, into pots on gravel in the greenhouse where they will grow tall and limber, freighted with fruit. Late August and September meant asters and goldenrod for the bees; now, the autumn flowers break in July, and we sow sea holly and mignonette, dill and bachelor's buttons and yarrow to stretch the season. The honeybees and bumbles seethe through this uncanny garden blossoming deep into October. Their wings are tattered and tired; they stutter and doze, worn out, replete.

III.

One for the mouse,
One for the crow,
One to rot,
And one to grow.

—*Old farmers' saying*

Seeding time is hope and loss, inextricable. Wolverine's Orca, Tiger's Eye, Hidatsa Shield Figure, Good Mother Stallard. I give the beans the best I can: warm soil on a fair day, plenty of water, birch brush for climbing. Ireland Creek Annie, Jacob's Cattle, Black Turtle. They will take their time underground, turning over against the June days like minuscule hourglasses, telling themselves their stories.

Nothing quells the energy of beans when they decide to grow, yet everything does: the smoke-filtered light, the soil's hard crust. The cotyledons drive and circle, shouldering against the clay pan like swimmers flailing under ice. Three times a day, I dip watering cans into the warm soup of the cistern, moisten the furrow over the beans' heads. If I have timed it right, the leaves will unfurl overnight like a parlour trick. In the early light of four a.m., I'll find myself called outside: the beans are above ground, only slightly late, carrying their stories with them into the still midsummer air.

IV.

July, interrupted. Fainting spells and seizures. Something has taken root, a pebble in my breast the size of a shelling pea. Seeds are not the only things whispering their stories: each day, the ache spreads, steals the strength from my arm. Over months of waiting in the anaesthesia of pandemic time, the tumour grows, shoulders to the surface of my skin, bulks quietly from shelling pea to the size of a hen's egg.

In illness, everything stops and keeps going at once. Imagine this body—a seed, clocking time, turned inward. Outside, the world tumbles over itself. I draw water, stack firewood, line the pantry with canning jars; inwardly, I listen, wonder if there is a way to recognize metastasis. Each throb in the bones, potential devastation.

The garden passes through asters, clocks goldenrod, highbush cranberry. It passes into early snow. Frost ambles through the plants at night, detonates in their cells like a pipe bomb.

I do not recognize my body, the wreckage of this garden.

V.

On the land, the work of your hands shapes a kind of love. Sowing, watering, and harvesting, but also cutting and clearing for better light, for smooth new growth. Pruning stills the tide of disease in old orchards, even if the heartwood has been touched.

A tended tree is a dance of thwarted urges. Look here: each pruning cut a redirection.

Each surgery, too, is a redirection. This one, and this one, and a further one still. The surgeon moves as quickly as he is able.

Chemotherapy. We salt the earth and hope for the best.

VI.

The cranes come back, and the tundra swans.
The garden answers in dandelions, in irrepressible chives.
The songbirds are fewer, and this is a kind of grieving.
My body is a landscape of seismic shifts, and this is a kind of grieving, too.

It is possible to hold hope and grief at once. It is the long span of waiting over a just-sown field, *one to rot and one to grow*, not knowing which will be which. It is the vigil over a body interrupted, fighting for its life in an interior space where no-one else can see.

This being human is not so far from a garden.
The deep, tender space in the bowl of the breast.
The rootlet of fear worried at like a tooth.
The hope that abides between grieving and anger.
The certain old sun and the balm of the moon.

Otherwise October

Scott Alderson

Please don't interrupt
my conversation
frustration situation
opportunity for idea exchange
after all anyway
I was trying to convey
a brighter day

please don't interrupt
my path my trail
madness prevails
nerves twitching body itching
like mite bites
after all anyway
I was struck by multiple sclerosis
and deep vein thrombosis

wish I could walk
leap jump without sound
but brain messages scramble
neurotransmitters interrupted
problems abound

please don't interrupt
my moment my life
no pause for strife
nerves twitching body itching
like mite bites.

Embolism Therapy

Alex Rettie

for Anna

"Breathe," I heard. "Breathe!" The monitor beside me beeped:
Fear stared out at me from eyes I didn't know.
I tried to gasp in air and failed. It hurt too much.
Then I saw you – patient and alert as we
Rehearsed some ancient violence and my lungs forgot
To fill. You smiled. A body of kindness. And
"Notice your breath now," you told me. "Notice your breath."
As far as I could bear the pain, I breathed it in.

Body I Dare You

Kufre Friesenhan

I

Some months ago, I stood by my window pondering the futility of dreams. My engorged breasts cried out for a baby to suckle their teats with no recourse. As I ached in all places feminine, my abdomen was an excruciating reminder of loss and of things that could have been. I realized that of things not present, my grief is never far away. It intruded and owned the space. Maybe it was a sight, maybe a smell. It was never really gone – for how could it go? Grief living was not a place I thought I would ever dwell in. It was running in my blood, just like pregnancy hormones, and taking its time. Food no longer tasted the same, sleep no longer came, and books held no promises of excitement. My sunken cheeks in the mirror and teary eyes whispered the untold stories I feared to put into words.

I remembered the slow steps towards the window, each step an electrifying jolt of pain. I was two weeks post-op and searching for answers as to how or why a once healthy placenta could fail. It was a silly question I returned to, again and again, even though the maternal and fetal specialists assured us these things were random and nobody really knew why. But I kept asking why. Did I do something wrong? Could I have inadvertently caused this?

II

I was submerged in a sea of grief with just the head poking out. I had lost my bearing. Lost to inconsolable agony, I floundered adrift. Sometimes

I wished to drown altogether. The current was pulling me in…and I sometimes flailed and writhed. Other times I lay perfectly still but not motionless because my inside tensed, tightened, and pulled on itself. The pain was intimate and agonizing, definite yet infinite, as it moved through and devoured every part of me. I moaned and whimpered.

I lost myself in the sea. Like a massive wave rolling in, my grief rose and fell in its arbitrary course until it reached the shore where it abandoned all that was within. There, it created pandemonium, and my body shattered into a hundred little pieces.

Standing at the window, I watched the chickadees dance around the bird feeder. Their movements reminded me that you cannot steady grief because it rocks and overthrows all inhibitions. It also sneaks up on you when you least expect it and unsettles everything.

III

We received the bird feeder right after our world collapsed and stopped. I remember thinking then, what a strange gift idea! I was a few days postpartum and barely able to walk upright. So, the partner set it up right where I could watch it from the lounge chaise for ease. I did not know, nor could I foretell that something so random could bring clarity and calm. It was not long before the birds gathered, or should I say the days bled into each other and I could not tell exactly how long it took for the birds to visit.

When you are in agony, the days can become a blur, a tasteless and languid routine you endure as punishment. But even that punishment was not enough. So, I starved myself. I loathed my body. I despised hugs and tenderness. I welcomed pain. I stared at myself in the mirror, my cheeks gaunt, eyes sunken. I sighed and went to sit on the sofa and watched the birds through the window with envy.

My mouth tasted sour. I became jealous of their apparent freedom, *joie de vivre*. I held my head and cried. I could not breathe. The partner ran to me from the bedroom and cradled me in his arms. Hyperventilating, I struggled to escape his embrace and failed. I nonetheless shared my feelings in four words, "I want my baby."

I was mad at everything around me.

IV

Some friends and family suggested another conception would help with the pain of loss, but I ignored them. Some said, with confidence, conceive again, and it would go smoothly. But how could they know? No one ever really knows with pregnancies, you see. And nobody warns you that life as you know it will never be the same again. As I slowly opened myself to the possibility of trying again, I did not consider that nothing could remain the same after such an earth-shattering experience.

It had been months, and I had spoken with a very understanding and kind grief counsellor. She asked that I take short walks outside the house for some fresh air. How do you say no to that? I found a way to, not because the weather was bad but because I was afraid my legs could buckle under me if I stood for too long. She never pushed but instead was full of understanding and praise. We talked every other day, but I mainly cried to her as I tried to articulate my feelings and thoughts. When she asked about school, I confided that I no longer wished to continue with graduate studies but was concerned that my family and friends might not understand. I was once again reassured that I did not need permission from friends and families to grieve in the ways I felt appropriate. And neither did I need permission to make decisions about my future.

I often asked, "When will I stop feeling miserable?" and she always gave the same reply: "You are on a journey, so focusing on the destination is a distraction from fully embracing the knowledge that each movement offers."

And she was correct. There was no schedule or calendar for grief. There was no right way or wrong way to grieve. Grief was as diverse as fingerprints, totally personal, and yet ubiquitous. The partner grieved in his quiet way, while I grieved with my heart on my sleeve, even as we held space and regularly spoke to one another about our feelings.

V

When we decided to try again, I could not foresee how quickly another pregnancy could manifest. I almost resented the ease. And I did not anticipate the new and strange phase of deep grief that followed. It was surreptitious yet overwhelming. When I suspected I could be pregnant, I was in disbelief for the first few weeks and incapable of happiness. I grudgingly went in to see the doctor and had no excitement for the recommended ultrasounds, which were crucial for this journey because of previous complications.

An atmosphere of sadness, anxiety, and doom covered my existence and crippled my expression. I could not share the news of how I was feeling with friends. I delayed the ultrasounds. No, I was not excited to see the heartbeat because experience says it can disappear without any warning. I thought I was being cautious because I now knew a lot more than the first time. This time around, I did not sing or play music to the belly like I had done the last time. I did not rub my growing belly like I used to. I did not caress and talk to it. I knew I should, I wanted to, but I was hobbled by fear and anxiety. The every-day-all-day sickness no longer brought warmth and hope because I feared it could all be in vain. I was hurting hard, in silence. I forgot pictures of the bump and failed to document its growth.

The bump did not get a name this time. Each day became a struggle, as if the days were unfolding slowly and nine months was far-removed. I failed to recognize the manifestation of grief. It was many months after and grief counselling had been paused because I was doing great. Or so we thought. My counsellor was happy when I emailed that I felt ready to try again. In her reply, she asked that I be mindful that each pregnancy journey was different and hold space for that. But how different? I did not think to ask. When it happened, it became clear that the pregnancy interrupted my grieving, or else grief was actively interrupting this precious and breathtaking experience of being pregnant, in ways I had never imagined.

And it was indeed a different experience. It was as if I were engulfed in an impenetrable gloom. I became overwhelmed with anxieties. I did not recognize that I mainly fed on the negatives of the past, not the rays of light it had brought into our lives, however briefly. My mind was incapable of looking forward to the hundred little exciting things that accompany pregnancies but instead focused wholly on the end: when I will hold my baby in my arms and leave the labour ward with her. After a successful first trimester, I did not share with friends and family that we were pregnant. The partner was forbidden from telling anyone. I became terrified of judgy and pitying looks. Most importantly, I was paralyzed with fear and frightened of failing my family and friends again.

There, I'd said it. I was afraid to be a failure again. Petrified, and emotionally paralyzed, I watched as the days rolled by. Days barely held meanings, as my only thought was my desire for the journey to attain a favorable outcome. But it had barely started.

VI

At seventeen weeks, a sharp, persistent, and intense pain in the lower right abdomen caused us some concerns, so we visited the obgyn. Although baby was doing fine, a detailed anatomy scan showed a thin uterine wall from the previous C-section. The doctor mentioned that I might not be able to take the baby to viability or full term. She said an evacuation might be called for if the pain intensified.

I was frozen in shock and horror. I was reminded that this was a high-risk pregnancy due to the previous placental failure. And now the thin uterine wall threw a wrench into an already murky situation. I was advised to be on bed rest and not exert myself beyond light chores.

But I broke down before I could control myself. We had a long discussion afterward about the dos and don'ts and the best possible ways to keep the baby and me safe.

And I instinctively cradled the bump in fear.

VII

As I stood by the long span window in a heated room, watching the snow fall and cover the world outside with a beautiful white layer, my body broke out in goose bumps. The tears rolled down my cheeks freely as I willed my body to not keel over like it tends to do— to keep holding on. I prayed for one more day. Then, I prayed for one more week and one more month, as I dared this weak body of mine to take us further.

My eyes drifted from the snow-covered lawns and parked cars to the lilac tree in front of the window. The chickadees and their dee-dee-dee sounds arrested my attention. They flew to the tree, perched, approached, and skirted around the bird feeder, and continuously pecked at the seeds. Some flew in, while others darted by. I spotted a robin, probably watching the commotion from the tree branch above, and waiting for her turn to dine. Some birds came, some flew away. As I watched their dance, I was transported to a time not so long before when I had watched the birds on the feeder and realized for the first time that grief, like the birds, comes and goes, ebbs and flows.

These days, grief returned to me like the black-capped chickadee that visited several storage spots for seeds cached throughout the seasons.

Would this also end in tears? I wondered.

X

Today, my therapist asks if I feel less anxious now that we are nearing 27 weeks, and I reply that we may not be safe even then. The birdcalls briefly interrupt my phone call. I cross the living room and stand by the window, listening to my therapist. I watch the snow fall, and my eyes flit to the bird feeder hanging from the lilac tree.

The chickadees and a blue jay joyously pick seeds from the bird feeder until a magpie arrives and sends them scattering in every direction with wingbeats and loud chirps. I smile at the brief racket and rub my belly.

"But does that not bring some form of comfort?" she asks.

"It does bring some comfort that we are nearing the mark of a viable preemie. But fear is never rational, you know. I think when overtaken with uncertainties, anxiety and fear are heightened till they drive comfort far away."

"Are you now taking bump pics?"

"Yes," I answer.

"Are you still talking to the baby?"

"Yes, I am. I told her just this morning how strong a fighter she is. She is helping me keep her safe. I could not do this without her help."

"Are you finding pockets of light and joy in this pregnancy"?

"Oh, absolutely I am. I would not trade it for any other experience."

Long after our call ends, I continue to watch the birds come and go. It is a beautiful sunny day in mid-March. The sky is bright and blue, the snow has begun thawing on the ground. The leafy scent of spring lurks in the air. Soon, the grass will be green again and the lilac tree in the front yard will bloom its sweet white flowers with alluring scents.

The birds continue dancing around the feeder and nearby branches. I am thinking of adding a bird bath outside. It is the least I can do for the coming summer. I have watched the birds' activities during moments of deep loss, profuse tears, gut-wrenching sadness, and ear-splitting wails.

But today, I watch them with hope, joy, and a smile. I wonder if, like me, they are anticipating spring when new life will burst forth. I crave hot chocolate, so I move lazily from the window to the kitchen to turn on the kettle.

And the baby kicks in response to my soothing movement. With every kick and tickle, she renews my strength and hope for a better tomorrow. The uncertainty that heralds each day now fills me with hope, not despair and dread.

I continue to pray for one more day, one more week, one more month.

"Keep holding on, little warrior," I whisper.

I applaud this body of mine for its greatness. I stand in that pocket of lightness and joy and embrace every broken and every whole part of me.

TRAUMA AND RETRIEVAL

Switch on The Night

Luciana Erregue-Sacchi

July 1, 1974:

HER EXCELLENCY, Vice President in charge of the Executive, Maria Estela Martínez de Perón, will direct a message to the Argentinian People. "To the Argentinian People: we are going through extenuating circumstances, which must redirect the Argentinian People towards a sense of true national unity. The President of the Argentines has given his country and the Latin American continent the most generous expression of generosity and Christian humanism. He sacrificed his life in search of peace for the People to his last breath. He worked tirelessly for our national, continental, and universal union. With enormous sorrow I must communicate to the People the passing of a true apostle of peace and non-violence, asking all citizens to make the necessary effort, within our national grief, to conduct the destiny of our nation towards the happy ending Perón dreamed for all Argentines. I pray friends and adversaries will set aside personal grievances and passions, towards a free, just, and sovereign nation. May God illuminate and fortify my commitment to the mission God and Perón commended to me."

February 20, 1975:

The house is an empty series of rooms. Two girls close to my age play between themselves; there are no toys, barely any furniture. A shell of a house. The curly-haired mother walks in the background between the rooms, she hardly interacts with her daughters. The dad's name is Gerónimo, or that is the name he goes by, according to my aunt, who has brought me here after dropping her daughter off at a friend's house. There are no introductions. Nobody knows who I am. I am at a table with Gerónimo and my aunt. Gerónimo is a dark, bearded man with a head full of jet-black hair, grave in his tone, serious in his demeanour. I look around, searching for normalcy, checking against the furniture in my own humble house, at least I have toys, unlike these girls. Why there are no toys? I speculate because they must be poor. But they do not look poor at all, the girls are lovely, maybe three and five years old. I am not sure what is going on, but I cannot think of anything except the lack of toys in that house. I feel sorry for the girls who do not seem to be doing much, other than talking to their mom. I do not feel, however, that anything is amiss, because I see a family, and being with my aunt means trusting an adult with the responsibility for my safety. And yet, the pit at the bottom of my stomach grows, especially because there is no food either. I feel completely disoriented, as if Maria Elena Walsh's song "El Reino del Revés" ("The Kingdom of Upside-Down,") a popular children's tune, has become part of our daily routines. Usually whenever we have visited friends' homes, at least we are welcomed with tea and stale biscuits. But this nothingness, this limbo, permeates my visits with my aunt, and those "special errands."

I am seven at the time and, like I do every summer, I get to spend a weekend at my cousin's house in La Plata. Her father is studying film, her mother has ostensibly returned to school to complete her high school degree. My aunt tells me we need to get her homework to Gerónimo. We walk a while, then we take a bus. Bored, I pick my nose at the table where Gerónimo and my aunt are chatting. He looks at me sternly and under his breath says: "Once I picked my nose and someone put a hot piece of metal up my nostril." Shocked at the violence in his voice, I recoil. This violence has the same air of brutality as my father's tales of bombings and kidnappings. My father patiently waits for the Sunday leftist paper, to cut out the editorials of the many guerrilla groups active in the country, and in La Plata, the city where he works. He laughs at their antics, such as the raising of their flag during a soccer game he attended with my four-year-old brother. I do not find Gerónimo's brutal way of speaking amusing at all.

Our next house visit is to a property consisting of a large succession of rooms, called *chorizo* style, or sausage homes. We stop at one. A pink glow welcomes us into the house, where a slim, "bronde" straight-haired young woman invites my aunt and me to sit on the floor as sitar music plays in her LP tray. Behind her is a wall hanging that looks like a pink, gold, and mauve mandala. She is wearing an off-white tunic. I am relieved she offers polite indifference to my presence. I spend the next twenty minutes just looking around. I leave that room enchanted. I forget the woman's name. It could have been Estela, or Adriana, or Cecilia. Those are the names of the prettiest twenty-something girls. I have never seen or heard about those friends of my aunt in my life. I used to know all of my aunts' friends. These ones, however, are entirely new, and one character more intriguing than the other. My aunt takes me for pizza and ice cream afterwards. No signs of my cousin, still at her friend's house for a sleepover.

People like my aunt, Gerónimo, and Estela, were a dime a dozen in the city of La Plata during the mid-seventies. They were part of leftist terrorist cells who distributed pamphlets and guns as they battled against the right-wing elements of their own party, the Triple A, whose men had riddled my aunt's house with bullet holes. For the adults in my life, my aunt's underground activities had never happened, therefore I believed them, until recently, when a friend of ours, visiting from Argentina, began reminiscing about those times. At dinner in our brand-new Edmonton kitchen, Jorge, also from the city of La Plata and a bit younger than my aunt and uncle, said, "I do not know why I am telling you this, but when I was doing my military service in La Plata, two of my fellow soldiers were kidnapped and tortured in a clandestine facility. They were involved in carrying pamphlets to leftist activists. Perhaps they were activists themselves." When I told him the story of Gerónimo and my aunt, he said "Those people existed, Luciana, and your aunt took you to an *aguantadero*, slang for clandestine guerrilla dwellings, I did operations in such houses." And he proceeded to enumerate all the houses they had been to, where guerrilla activists were then detained, or died by suicide, leaving their children behind. I had been taken along for the ride as my aunt conducted her illegal activities, behind her family's back. My aunt presented as the angelic Liv-Ullman-like aunt who loved children more than anything in the world.

Staying at my aunt's house was always a complicated affair to navigate for an overprotected country bumpkin like me. My aunt and her then-husband lived on the outskirts of the big city, surrounded by highways. They were adored by their neighbours, the produce shop owner, the butcher, the policeman next door. My aunt's house was a folly, designed by her husband. It had Spanish stucco walls, terracotta tiled floors in the kitchen and dining area, synthetic carpet flooring in the bathroom (the kind used in office spaces) and an entirely orange bathroom with pink shower curtains and lighting. You could say it might have been inspired by an acid trip or the Beatles' Sergeant Pepper Album or both. I enjoyed my visits there, although they had a dog, Fedra, a chill Saint Bernard that terrified me. My aunt was never home at the time. Even though she was a stay-at-home mom, she would leave the house in the morning and return at noon to feed us a hastily made lunch of beef or hotdogs and fries.

When my cousin and I woke up in her room, filled to the brim with dolls and posters of blonde children, Khalil Gibran and Saint Exupéry quotes, the Little Prince looking over us, instead of the crucifix like the one adorning all the bedrooms at my parents' home, we would make ourselves breakfast on the messy kitchen island. My aunt's bed was always unmade, chaotic, unlike my parents' bed. My cousin's father would spend hours locked up in his studio, concocting film screenplays, arranging dates with actors, musicians, and photographers. His own father, a Spanish Civil War refugee, ran the hardware store downstairs and was seemingly the only adult to give the children the warmth they were not receiving from their young parents, too busy with their own activities. His whole life fitted into a cupboard-like room in between the kitchen and the living room, and it was full of black and white photos of his wife, dead soon after giving birth to my uncle.

After that visit to Gerónimo's and the unusual stay at my aunt's I called my father's work and asked to be picked up. Once I was home, I told my mom, in tears, "I do not want to go there anymore, this is not a family." I was so relieved to be safe at my house, which was my grandparents' house, with family dinners every night and four meals a day sitting at a table, that I forgot to tell them about Gerónimo.

Once home, safely away from my aunt and Gerónimo, I would go back to enjoying my leisurely Saturday afternoons reading the book my parents had gifted me to celebrate my good grades, Ray Bradbury's *Switch On the Night*, a children's book translated as *La Niña que Iluminó la Noche*.

March 24, 1976
Comunique Nº 1:
We communicate to the population that as of today, the country is under the operational control of the Junta of General Commanders of the Argentinian Armed Forces. We recommend to all citizens strict acquiescence to the directives emanating from the Military, Police, or Security Authority, as well as extreme care to avoid actions or individual or group attitudes and activities that may demand the drastic intervention of the operational personnel.

August 26, 1976:
One might think the calendar turns the same way for everyone. Not in my family. To paraphrase George Lakoff, our birthday celebrations varied in the fineness of their grain. They were, more often than not, non-events that had to happen. Ever since I learned to write, I would hand-make invitations with construction paper unevenly trimmed with the old, blunt scissors—my parents did not trust me with the sharp ones—and quietly deliver them to my friends at school.

My birthday was always in August, the middle of winter in Argentina. It was always bone-chilling and gloomy. At home, birthday entertainment always fell on the shoulders of the birthday girl or boy, we would all be left to our own devices. As the guests arrived, each would hand a gift to us, and we would immediately open it and pass it around for the rest of the group to admire and play with, before Mom caught wind of it and removed it from our sight. Consistently, all the girls would dress in their finest attire, frilly dresses, or plaid skirts and blouses or turtlenecks, patent leather or suede Mary Janes, and sometimes, even a little purse, "for your handkerchief," the moms would say. As the years progressed, we would move on from playing tag and hide and seek to staging fashion shows reminiscent of Paris is Burning, inventing award and punishment categories, such as "best walk with your toes inward" or "best side-parted hairstyle."

If you left it up to my mother, birthday party preparations would involve baking a packaged cake, halving it, and slathering dulce de leche everywhere, then grabbing a toy doll, slapping on some cornflakes and the requisite candles et voilà, the birthday cake of your dreams—or nightmares—was ready and stored on grandma's cupboard until the guests arrived. Every time we had a birthday at home, the woman who helped my mother around the house would mysteriously fall ill. I remember my mom stressing about how Justina had failed to show up. It would be an all-out frenzy to open the bags of chips and snacks, inflate the balloons, and get the plastic cups and paper napkins on the dining table just in time to receive our friends.

On August 26, 1976, my grandparent's checkered hallway, aka the dance floor, filled with twenty or thirty children jumping up and down to The Beatles' "It's Been a Hard Days Night" and "She Loves You," shaking our bodies, purposefully stepping on balloons to hear them pop, as my newborn brother slept soundly in the room next door, a mere month after the soldiers had entered my house searching for subversive materials.

April 2, 1982:
National Radio One, Buenos Aires, Argentina, and LS 82, Channel 7, Argentina Colour Television broadcasts directly from Government House. Military Junta Communiqué: As the Supreme Organ of the State, the Military Junta communicates to the people of the Argentinian Nation that today the Republic, through its Armed Forces, accomplished its most successful mission. A coordinated operation resulted in the recovery of the Malvinas, Georgia and South Sandwich Islands, for our national territory, guaranteeing the exercise of Argentinian sovereignty over the territory of the aforementioned islands and their corresponding maritime and flying zones. It behooves the entire country to understand the deep and unequivocal sense of national sovereignty behind this decision. We know collective responsibility and effort will accompany this endeavour and will allow us, through the help of God, to transform and legitimize this reality, so that the neglected Argentinian people will be rewarded for their patience after almost 150 years of abuse. National Radio One, Buenos Aires, Argentina, and LS 82, Channel 7, Argentina Colour Television have broadcasted directly from Government House to all other channels and radio stations of our National Broadcasting Network.

Soon after my fourteenth birthday my mother casually began dropping hints that this was going to be a momentous year in my life. "How would you like to have a nice fifteenth birthday party, Luciana?" My teenage brain did not compute the significance of the number or my mother's zeal for such a celebration. I saw photos of her own quinceañera party, a small, yet classy family affair, my grandparents, her brother, and her closest aunt and cousins, all toasting with champagne flutes, and a cake. My mom in a white full skirt dress, her hair in a short, wavy bob with super short bangs, as 'fifties fashion required, photo smiles, no friends around, the piano my grandfather had gifted her occupying pride of place in the dining room. The painting of the sailboat braving a storm, in the background, like my grandmother's brain operation that year. "Why is turning fifteen so important compared to fourteen or sixteen?" I would moan this question everywhere I went, sabotaging my mom's attempts for me to enter my small town's "polite society."

"We will go to Chela, the dressmaker, next week," was her answer. Amidst all this excitement, the Falklands War was declared. What followed were endless trips to Chela's house, under the April rain, or the winter darkness of July 1982 after 5:00 pm. This was no ordinary darkness, the streetlights in my town were turned off as per the request of the national military in case English aircraft decided to blanket our town of 15,000 with bombs. We would trudge the darkened streets once my mom finished work, or after her Saturday hair appointments, where, step by step, she would broadcast to the assembled ladies the preparations for the party. My friends and I would stop by the train station, with care packages to hand out to the soldiers leaving for the south of the country, to fight a war they had not anticipated even two months before. They were a mere couple of years older than us. We would ask the names of the best-looking ones, a useless task before the age of social media, a way to make the imaginary, real. British music was banned, no more Beatles for birthday parties, only Argentinian rock, like Charly García's "Do not Bomb Buenos Aires" or throwback music from the early seventies. As it turned out, the musicians banned by the same dictatorship that had started the war were now the only performers we could listen to on FM radio.

As for my mom, the battle was just beginning. She would sell gold jewelry, ask her mother-in-law for money, and request discounts and favours from relatives and friends. I got to choose the invitations, the dress, the shoes, and the young guests. My parents would choose the rest. I entered the party on my father's arm, with a song titled "Cinderella" by Argentinian singer Nito Mestre echoing through the corridor of the nightclub owned by my uncle Carlos. The club was specially decorated for the event with branches of plum blossoms my mom had plucked from the acreage of a now-disgraced minister of education whose house had been bombed at the beginning of the dictatorship. The photographer did such a great job, apparently, that the photo album of my *quince* visited the households of my younger girlfriends, like the effigy of the Virgin Mary, as proof that miracles existed.

Like the visit with Gerónimo, the book my parents gifted me, *Switch on the Night*, had disappeared from my life. I never heard my aunt mention that name again, the book was no longer in our library. The memories became dubious. Did all of this happen or were the memories mere interruptions of a perfectly normal and boring small-town childhood? After all, my mom would always comment "Luciana, you are always so febrile!"

I buried these memories for a quarter century, mostly because I could not make sense of them. One day I casually told the memories to my mom—the one who thinks I am febrile—twenty-five years after the fact. She confirmed my suspicions that it had not all been a figment of my imagination, adding "What do you want with your aunt, she was—and still is—a flake!" Growing indignant, she exclaimed: "How could she have done that to you and to us? We knew nothing!"

There is so much more I am still trying to come to terms with, that when people poke and prod for yet more precision, and ask, "How did things feel to you as a child?" I can only respond that if you are a trauma survivor, you know that some things you simply cannot remember. The brain has worked hard to protect you so you could grow into a functioning adult. All the immediacy I can provide is the book. I found *Switch on the Night* this year, at the Buenos Aires Book Fair, and I hastily purchased it, finally recognizing myself in that girl, switching on the night. The book sits now on my bedside table, tangible evidence of those dark times. As for my fifteenth birthday party aftermath, by August 1982, the war against Britain would be lost, as we enjoyed my birthday cake, a Welsh fruitcake with chocolate chunks covered in the purest white fondant, made by the wife of a British friend of my family's.

'skwesis(ak), interrupted

Meghan Eaker

Black robes and white coats pace
the hallway of her quivering spine.
Their antiseptic voices seek to purify,
and she is unclean.

Sober now, she suffers in the hangover
of Social Darwinism. Suckled on beliefs borne
before her, she doubts the fitness of

her own birth. Interrupted
before begun, she swats at the thoughts
that swarm her consciousness.

Call her crazy!
She feels disinherited truths.

From the cradle of their interrupted girlhoods,
generations of 'skwesisak spring up unwholly.

Unfit for this world, in fragmented moments,
they craft another.

Note to the reader:

iskwesis is the nehiyawewin (Cree) word for girl. iskwesisak is the plural form. When pronounced by many fluent speakers the words sound like 'skwesis and 'skwesisak.

Snow Gait

Shazia Hafiz Ramji

a language so old   my hand goes to my rib
remembering a new pain   shine on flesh   then a voice
in my headphones says   she was stabbed   just under
the heart   a language so old   these names   throated
a fist in a trunk   a memory of the girl who was made
to disappear so that when I remember her story
all I remember is trees and my family's soft steps
on wet rocks   across the river   shiny comets
of Kilimanjaro snow like the gait of luck
or my father's kindness   my heart is so big
here   it has returned with the aspen that claps
so that light is always a verb it bounces
gilds   stills
and I seek the moon scrambled in black ice
I ask for the girl I used to be absenting
herself   at the shore for no reason at all
waiting for lights to signal   from a distance
as if there was an elsewhere to look forward to
as if that elsewhere was not now   just to remember
the vantage point was the wish
it came to me in the face of a stranger I was sure was kin
a language so old   a mirror of myself
like siblings who know they are in pain
far away   my past self in that face
wound upon wound
whipped thoughts like a three-headed dog
but snow shuffles your footprints

out of its seams snow cuts no borders
snow makes the grass river this gift
when it comes is snow because
you have to be whole to see
the root in the mirror
to like what you see
then break
an interruption
this is how you return
to your life choosing against the person
that was your face following the amniotic
wish a language so old there is no question
only prayer:
to leave without hurting
anyone to be grateful for this unmooring
this knowing this trust
in the witness of blood.

My Father's Left Ear Has Been Hurting for Thirty Years

Uchechukwu Peter Umezurike

My father's left ear hurts.

He tells me to look in
the canals of his ear
which he hardly cleans.

He says there is a footpath
snaking up
a bombed-out village
before the market where
oranges wilt
in baskets

like dreams
forgotten

meat rots
on sunlit slabs

the lamb's guts
around which
blowflies rally

past the river
where bodies
chewed in bits by fish
bloom hyacinths

by the church

dim with silences
whose bells
no longer speak
in tongues

down the civic hall
where a rank of rats
now preside
over hope.

My father's ear hurts;

I find nothing there
even as I squint.

My father insists again
that I look.

Look inside!

Can you not see
the zinc sheets
screaming?

Can you not see
the bullets
roasting flesh?

Can you not see
families fleeing
a legion of rifles?

Do you not see
earth convulsing
under a babel of footfalls?

No, father. I am sorry.

I don't see anything.

Have you no eyes? my father snaps
his knuckles
concrete
and familiar
like the scars
on his thigh.

Look!
You should at least
see the hairless birds
with featherless necks
dancing around
a wounded soldier.

I squint harder.

Wax as a wound is all I see.
I don't tell him
knowing
his anger is a bull
yanked by his horn.

I exclaim
like a child prophet
pacing the street:

There are clouds in your ear, father,
trapped
but thundering.

HUMAN AND NON

Industrial Door

Marco Melfi

Uniformed in charcoal. Push-bar belted.
Cinder blocks' cousin. Its dolley-kicked
shins mimic a Jackson Pollock. Quick
to shut and stubborn about fire suppression.
A slam known to interrupt a foreman's
orders or a fork-lift's warnings.
Coughing for fresh air? Find the front entrance.
Carts to unload? Haul them to the dock.
Like an arms-crossed guard, approach it
only in emergencies. Rookies will learn
of its weight in this warehouse on smoke
breaks: their bottles, jammed to prop open
a finger's grip gap, will get chopped.

The Bull

Micheline Maylor-Kovitz

Bless the bull
who unhooks the latch
on the metal door
of the livestock truck
to loose the hinge
escape the gate,
step out of the fate
of the abattoir truck
to run amok
in the town's
tuck shops
to gore the woman
her husband too
for horning in
for taking a ride
round the little shop
with bric-a-brac stacks
of this-and-that.
Bless that bull
for carpe-ing his diem.

In my own china shop,
of living,
I'm just living
as if time
isn't hauling me
to end times
as if there's time

for glue
and kintsugi,
as if every untouched
broken thing
in my spare room,
as if time
has time to spare.

This land via artefact
(or situating ourselves on this stolen land)

Moni Brar

Let us interrupt our story, reconsider this façade,
and read the land.
What does this stand of aspen say? How do we respond
to this heat, bent and bowed to the tree's trunk?
To this tree ring, this crack in earth's surface,
this thin-veined tendril clinging?
This line where mountain meets sky, this line of shadow,
line of skin on soil?
This curved line of, the straight line to,
the heart of a pinecone ever turning?
The wavy lazy line of the river,
hard-edged line of cliff and fall?
The razed line of burnt forest,
the line between bee and nectar bloom?
How do we hold this line on palm of hand on soiled heart?

—

Pick wild saskatoons in the damp brush. Thank each berry for the stained imprint it gifts your hands that have done so much damage. See the stories hidden in the grasses? The grasses that will be woven into baskets to hold children with stories already tucked in their mouths. Each day a remembrance, fleeting as the hares across the snow.

—

No. You do not have to ask. You do not have to wait to say, *is there something I can do*?

The weeds need recognition. The fences need removal. The sky needs holding up.

—

Staunch your rabid heartbeat,
your ribbed grief.
These verdant fields, this gleaning oak,
this soft-tipped moon before it dives into the ocean,
were never ours.
The sun will continue to polish limbs,
darken the skin of fruit,
while something is quietly pruned out of us.
It is needed.

REBUILDING

Quicksilver

Thea Bowering

Aisling said okay, she would give the interview. It was for a man who once tried to kiss her neck without invitation. Long ago he had published a small book of poetry by her father; he knew her father, ergo, he could kiss her neck. She was going to meet with him anyway, since he was the only one who'd shown an interest in talking to her about her novel. She pinned her hair into a loose chignon, then took it down. She wasn't sure how to dress, if there would be a photo. She tried on the threadbare (now vintage) Mr. Peanut t-shirt her father had been reluctant to hand over, even though it hadn't fit him in decades. Her bra showed through a bit. She added her black Hugo Boss jacket—peaked pagoda shoulder and slim in the arms, bought with a friend's discount.

When she arrived at the downtown pub, the interviewer was already there. He looked the same as he had when he'd tried to kiss her neck. Long peach-coloured hair combed straight back, round gold-rimmed glasses, a silly little moustache. She knew him from the West Coast, but he'd recently moved to Alberta to become editor of an important arts magazine. He was relentlessly hard working, known largely for his interviews with Canadian writers. Any Canadian writer would take an interview with him, but most would be surprised to hear he'd snagged the gig at the magazine. His smile faded when he saw Aisling come through the door. Although his face might simply be responding to hers. She hadn't thought about what to do with her face.

As soon as she sat down, he began asking questions. Ones about her influences, of course. "Oh well, lately Lucia Joyce." Aisling wasn't going to say her father. She was reading a biography about James Joyce's daughter who had been moved recklessly around the fantasy world of her alcoholic parents until her brother, Giorgio, put her into an asylum for throwing a chair at her mother, Nora.

"Everyone thought her 'despair' was keeping her father from completing *Finnegan's Wake*. But really, she was institutionalized to get her out of the way. Joyce was distressed by this," Aisling made a dismissive gesture, "but he was swift at getting women out of the way. Just ask Sylvia Beach."

Gold Glasses said he didn't know Joyce had a daughter who wrote.

"She didn't write. Well, not really." Aisling stared at his face. She had forgotten how wet and red his lower lip got. "She was a dancer. Strange, modern dance. She wore a beaded headpiece and moved in Egyptian poses." Aisling bent her wrists and jutted both hands quickly to the right. "Only her father 'got' her dancing. In an interview she gave from the asylum, where she died by the way, in the interview she said her life now was 'just as if you had been very rich, and collected many valuable things, and then they were taken away from you.' I liked that." She emptied her glass. The server passed by, and Aisling raised her arm, indicating she would like another, and some yam fries. She wondered who was paying.

"She was screwed over by her family. I mean her soul was. And Joyce knew it. Her family destroyed all her letters, so we'll never really know anything." Aisling smoothed down her staticky hair as she talked.

"Any actual writers who inspired you early on ... or just dancers?" Gold Glasses asked. He really was an a-hole, wasn't he.

"Maeve Brennan, I guess." He wouldn't know who that was, either.

"She came to America from Dublin in the thirties. A teenager. When her parents went back, she stayed. Lived in hotels around Manhattan, by herself. She wrote for The New Yorker, funny sketches about people on the street. A dream job. Always well-dressed, well made-up. She wasn't married, well, only briefly. She liked animals," Aisling told him. "I've always liked writers who seem like orphans," she added.

"Which is not unlike being an only child, like yourself," he gestured towards her, palm-up, as though she were a prize.

"She probably drank too much," Aisling looked away. "People started noticing she was a little unkempt in public. Later in life she wandered the streets, hotel to hotel. Sometimes they found her asleep in the washroom at The New Yorker. Funnily enough," Aisling waved a yam fry, "her first and most famous story was about an ageing hotel-bathroom attendant—she tries to keep her job by divulging the secrets of her co-workers. It backfires on her. She loses everything." Aisling dipped the fry in aioli. "She ends up dying alone, ward of the state."

"Sad," Gold Glasses offered.

"I admire her commitment to writing, and how she was alone in the world." Aisling shifted back and forth on her stool, placed her elbows on the vinyl tabletop, then took them away. "To break from the past, family, blindly follow one's destiny. It's what you have to do. It's like hiding little brightly coloured envelopes, in public, that perhaps no one will ever find."

Glasses said he had no idea what she meant.

For some reason, Aisling began telling him about the moment during her childhood when she discovered her "authentic self" (her mother's term). It happened one day while she was playing alone along the stone, medieval-looking wall that wrapped around the corner-lot of her home. She ran inside to the deep drawer that held ribbons and paper used for parties and holidays. She found some miniature envelopes that came in vivid colours: red, yellow, blue, and purple. She shook all the silver out of her glass piggybank, separated the dimes, nickels, and quarters, and put different amounts into each little envelope. A yellow one got four quarters. A red one, eight. Blue got only a dime and a nickel. Then she sealed them. Then she went back out to the street and began hiding them under the ivy that trailed along the capping stones of their garden wall, and between the exposed mossy roots of the hundred-year-old chestnut trees on the boulevard. She thought: what a nice surprise it would be for people who were observant enough—to catch sight of a bit of colourful paper poking out here and there, as they walked along, acting out their daily routines. Some of the envelopes might not be found for years. People would be baffled and wonder how they got there. Was it fairies? Who would do such a thing? She was the master of fortune! This idea had brought her such extreme joy that she began to think about the future. What she might be by then, what she could do.

"But then it struck me—who *would* do such a thing?" Aisling placed her narrow hand flat on the tabletop and spun her body towards Gold Glasses.

"Someone who did not know how to be anything in life. Someone who would never find a career like her friends would, like the grownups she knew had. She wouldn't have children, or love, or a house of her own. She would live in spaces she happened to find herself in, with no means or real desire to leave them. Someone who had not been born into poverty, but who had not been taught to want money, either, or how to acquire more. Someone who just couldn't see how it all added up."

Gold Glasses was studying her face.

"This person would only ever have occasional, disconnected moments of happiness, flashes of colour. Nothing else. No plan." Perhaps all the people walking by with purpose had missed the bright paper altogether, until it turned white and melted away in the coastal rain, leaving nothing but a bare, random quarter.

Gold Glasses asked if she thought it was a generational thing.

Aisling excused herself and slid off the stool.

In front of the bathroom mirror she pulled a silver bullet-shaped lipstick from her pocket and popped the top. She dug deep into the tube with her pinky and reapplied the creamy nude tone. What was she doing? In her head was a self-created scene based on a news story that had ended the career of the country's most beloved literary satirist. It came to her faintly from time to time. The woman is being held up by her throat in a stairwell. The stairwell is very modern: white, glass, and chrome. The woman, less clear— she was a fan, and had sent the author a sexy email the next day. Not uncommon. Aisling had once let a guy finish, then scribbled down her real number before realizing what had happened. That's not completely true; she had switched to playing dead about halfway through, like you do with a bear. Lying there, she had thought about a scene near the end of Joyce's story, "The Dead," in which the husband looks at his wife and thinks of all the private moments of their life together. Ones he wants to make her recall, ecstatic ones that break through the dullness *like the tender fire of stars.*

Aisling washed her hands and discovered the bathroom was out of brown paper towel. She should tell the server. There were two bins below the empty dispenser. One said 'landfill' and the other 'recycling.' They were filled about even. She went back out to the table.

He was fiddling with his mini recorder.

"A few of us are on the side of the dead," she said.

"Okay," said Gold Glasses. "Let's proceed."

—

He asked her if she'd ever gotten feedback about her writing from her father. "Oh yes, of course." This was the thing he was after. Aisling broke the paper ring from her bundle of cutlery as though it were a Christmas cracker and blotted her fingers with the napkin.

She told him about the time she was eighteen, carrying her first finished story out in front of her towards the TV room where her father sat in front of the ball game. As usual, he was still in his pajamas— expensive burgundy silk, the hem torn practically right off. Her mother had bought them several birthdays back. She bought him beautiful pajamas every year, until she died.

"He always sat in the same way. I can see it clearly," Aisling looked towards the ceiling. "Casually crossed legs, an ankle bone sticking out between his jammy bottom and his slipper. Eyebrows raised, and his hand

(Aisling demonstrated with her long palm) wrapped around the whole lower half of his face as he's reading his magazine or doing the crossword."

Gold Glasses was scribbling furiously now.

Aisling continued. "He put down Sports Illustrated, or Quill & Quire, or whatever it was, and read my story during the commercial breaks while I sat there. When he was finished, he had two comments. The first was that I had misquoted his poem in my story. 'It fell like quicksilver. I would never say felt in a poem.' The second was that he envied the last line." This had thrilled her. This was the moment she knew she could be a writer. "The tables turn on the narrator in the last line," Aisling drew a quick circle on the tabletop. "The two lovers of the story go off and enjoy their lives, while the narrator's left alone at the bar, scribbling down words."

The interviewer stops writing. He mentions the avant-garde group her father was part of when he was young and asks if her style is influenced by them. That idea of "a walking voice."

"I make observations as though I am crossing a busy street and ignoring an ambulance coming through—"

The interviewer puts the cap on his pen, says he guesses he will quote this for the magazine. Aisling says she got the idea from a scene in a French New Wave film. A man and a woman in the foreground are talking about their personal problems, oblivious to the crowd slowly gathering behind their backs around some accident you can't quite see. She thought it was a cool image to riff on—

"That should do it," says the interviewer.

Aisling stands up. The interviewer grins at her, gives her a hug, his round glasses opaque in the bar light. She asks if maybe she can see it, before it goes to print. She hesitates, then puts down some money for the beer and fries. She leaves the pub and begins to walk. Heavy limbs. Marbles for eyes. Like one of Baudelaire's ladies, she thinks. The ghost of something strange and guilty ...

—

Standing at the last light before home, Aisling considers an ambulance slowing in the near distance. It noses its way into the wide intersection and then stops as the final cars criss-cross in front of it. They look like colourful little toys against the snow. One ... two ... three ... she counts the seconds shaved off, crucial to the person hurt inside. She steps down into the street.

When the long panel passes close to her face, for a moment everything is a dull white— then one leg bends comically, and her hair lifts, surprised, into the air.

Baby Interrupted

Teresa Wouters

I used to sit on the pity pot. I had a lot to feel sorry for. Raised in Edmonton, I knew its streets well because I practically lived on them. I was so dirty and tough looking that I scared people. One time I sat at the back of a public bus and didn't notice that everyone was moving to sit far away from me until a man got on and started to walk towards the many empty seats that surrounded me. Back then, I shielded myself from hate, abuse, and neglect behind the metaphorical wall that I had surrounded myself with. It was the invisible wall where I could throw invisible bricks at the world. When I looked the man in the eye, he stopped with sudden force, like he had just come face-to-face with a hungry grizzly. I watched his widening eyes fixed on me and his face paling. His display of fear and weakness fed me with a desire to attack, but he turned and took a seat with the others up front. I was the poster child for anger, resentment, and abandonment.

After a year of shutting out the world with Pink Floyd's "The Wall" album streaming through my headphones, I decided to tear down the wall. In an effort to better myself, I showered and put on clean clothes and devoted myself to doing better in school. From kindergarten on, school was a disaster for me. I couldn't do math, I didn't know how to write a research paper, an essay, or even a proper sentence. Maybe I can blame my elementary teachers who put students in rows according to their last names. Which means that I was always in the back of the class because my last name started with a W. In front of me sat a colourful garden of bright, happy students. The teacher was the sun, orbiting across the front of the room, feeding her blooming children with nutritious facts and complimentary sunshine.

I sat in their shadows. Invisible and forgotten. Wilting. Elementary report cards identical with the lowest passing grade and a comment: Teresa can do better. My parents, teachers, even peers said I was dumb. During this year of trying to better myself, I asked my math teacher for help on a problem.

He said, "If you can't figure that question out by yourself then you must really be stupid." He left his desk to help a smarter student. It had taken about twenty minutes to talk myself into having the courage to walk past all the other kids, and in seconds my favourite teacher shredded me into pieces in front of everyone. This was the one teacher I thought would save me. The one who could finally help me pass after trying and failing the lowest class for math. He was right. I was too dumb for school. I walked out and never returned.

I got fired from McDonalds because the boss accused me of stealing from a co-worker's purse. The co-worker showed him that nothing was stolen. How could he fire me right after hanging out at my house on Saturday where he tried to make some moves on me. I tried retail where a thirty-three-year-old saleswoman was jealous that I could outsell her. One of my customers was about to pay for a pile of clothes that I helped her pick out. I was about to ring up the purchases when my jealous co-worker walked up to us and said, "All those clothes look ugly on you."

The customer walked out.

I quit.

I escaped to the bars, drinking with shadows of other people. We sat stoned in our own dark worlds where intoxicating drinks, booming dance music, and twirling lights confused us into a fantasy of clinging one-nights of love and friendships. Only to wake in a hung-over fog of defeat, loss, and helplessness.

At twenty-two, I became pregnant.

Ooops.

Yes, my life was miserable. Poor, unsupported, uneducated, with low job skills, I had a lot to feel sorry for, and I got into the habit of telling everyone I met about it. Until a pregnant, heroin addict prostitute who had recently been released from jail for committing an armed robbery with her boyfriend who had later killed himself said to me, "Quit your whining!" Her comment was a shock to my system. It carried me over the threshold of new experiences that changed my life.

Anyone who attempts to become a better person will come across messages and lessons of strength, clearing vision, bravery in the face of adversity, ambitious attempts at climbing the highest mountain after clawing out of the deepest abyss.

Maybe I didn't have a lot to feel sorry for after all. Being pregnant gave me a choice. I could either hang out with my nowhere crowd, or I could dump them to be a parent. I dumped my nowhere crowd.

Having a baby to care for changed my life forever because I wanted to give my daughter a better life than the one I'd had so far. It was my vow to her. But I didn't know how.

One day, a man wandered into my world. He looked out of place in his salesman suit and confident smile. He pointed his gaze at me and came at me like an arrow shot from a bow. He had targeted me on purpose. In a maze of plastic chairs and tables sat groups of chattering people. I was the one person sitting slouched and alone, a sad-sack of misery and hopelessness. Joe saw me as a person without a purpose and he wanted to give me one. He sat down and introduced himself while trying to start some friendly conversation in an attempt to get me to trust him. Joe had all the confidence in the world, and in his best saintly voice, asked, "What do you want to do with your life?"

I shrugged, "I don't know."

With patience and care, he prodded out of me some of my interests. I mumbled that I liked writing, drama, animals, and the outdoors., "That sounds like some skills that a teacher should have," he said. "Would you like to become a teacher?"

I shrugged and said, "I don't know."

Joe talked to me about life skills and jobs skills and academic upgrading. If I wanted to reach any type of goal, he said, I had to take the first step. Through Joe and his co-worker, Bev, I was put into the first pilot project for Edmonton's Life Skills programs. Most of the students were currently in halfway houses and rehab programs or homeless. We participated in developing life skills, conflict management skills, and even employment skills. The instructors gave me competency tests that told them I was very smart. A lifetime of being told that I was dumb was too etched in me, so I didn't believe them. Joe and Bev sent me to an upgrading school for adults like me. Every morning, as I got off the downtown bus and walked to the office building where my classes were held, I had to endure the presence of a man who walked on the opposite side of the street whistling "Jesus Loves Me." Maybe he was an angel to guide me towards my destination.

Attending an adult school was so much easier than my trials and suffering in the institution called high school. I got to work at my own pace. My first challenge was trying to pass a low-academic course that I had called Dummy Math in high school. In high school, I had tried four times to pass that Dummy Math course, each time destroying my textbook in frustration and failing. But this time, in adult upgrading class, I finished it in two weeks. I got 93%. On to the next level of math! I finished in six days with another mark of 93%. Maybe I wasn't so dumb after all. Other courses were in classes with supportive instructors and friendly students. As I passed course after course, an advisor encouraged me to go to university.

I took the tour of the University of Alberta, but after about an hour, I slipped away from the group, tears welling in my eyes. I had always wanted to go to the University of Alberta, but the other people in the tour group were dressed better than me, they looked intelligent and confident and pretty, and they all seemed to have their act together and...they were better than me.

I couldn't go there; I just didn't belong.

My advisor suggested the University of Lethbridge. At the time, it had a reputation for graduating the best teachers.

Another new experience? It would mean moving away from the city that I had always lived in, the people I knew, the security of familiar streets. I wrote a very personal letter to the university's administration office. The letter was tear-soaked when I wrote it. I had filled the paper with pleading words, begging them to accept me as a poor, young, single parent, so that I could give my baby daughter a better life.

Wow. It worked. They actually let me in as a mature student (someone over 22 years old who hadn't graduated from high school).

At the end of August, I got off a Greyhound bus in the middle of the town of Lethbridge. I looked up the street, then turned and looked down the street. I did not know which way to go. I asked a passerby, "Where is downtown?"

He said, "You're standing in it." I looked up and down the street at the businesses. There were no towering buildings. This was the first day of an entirely different life.

My time at the University of Lethbridge was full of new trials and suffering that strengthened my soul, cleared my vision, inspired my ambitions, and helped me to achieve successes that I could never have imagined gaining if I had stayed in Edmonton.

Yet, I didn't know that I couldn't write one straight sentence, nor did I have any study skills. The university threatened to kick me out because I was borderline illiterate. I had a choice. I could drop out—but I didn't want my daughter to have a failed mother. Or I could do something about my skills deficit.

I did something about it.

I sought out people I admired to become my role models, I learned how to study, I took writing courses and partnered with students who got As. I gained confidence in speaking in classrooms filled with hundreds of students. People complimented my opinions. The more I got involved, the more people wanted to know me. I could now look people in the eye and enjoy new friendships. I felt that I belonged.

My marks went from bad to good to great. I graduated with a Bachelor of Arts. I did it!

Two years later, my six-year-old daughter never took her eyes off me as I crossed the stage to receive my Bachelor of Education degree. I had become my daughter's role model.

My parents came to Lethbridge to attend my B.Ed. graduation. This was the first time they'd travelled to Lethbridge to see me After the ceremony, my dad said, "We thought you were lying about being in university."

I moved back to Edmonton and caught up with some old friends, the same ones I had known as a teenager. However, I got some odd reactions. My friends were telling me what to do. They interrupted my sentences, my suggestions were swept aside, and they insulted and patronized me. They were especially angry when I called them on their rude behavior towards me. I had to stop being their friend. I had changed, they hadn't. It seemed that they saw my new confidence and university degree as a threat to their own feelings of low confidence and failure. Maybe they'd also had a lifetime of messages that they were too dumb and not good enough.

For myself, I have learned that whining and sitting on the pity pot is an absolute no-no. Worrying is fine, in small doses, as long as I can kick myself in the butt and ask myself what I'm going to do about it.... and then, do something about it. Change bad thinking habits. Be bold enough to step into new worlds. That is the only way to overcome any obstacle that life puts before me. I can fill my life with as many moments and experiences of joy and passion as humanly possible. The key has been to start with one experience and build on it. And my greatest ongoing experience has been to develop the belief that I can accomplish anything I desire to do. I control my own choices.

Having a baby was a gift. She became my inspiration and my motivation. I flushed away the pity-pot and became the best version of me.

Image Drop

Katherine Koller

I'm a girl with long hair, often in a ponytail to my mid-back.

I never question the term *ponytail* until I'm on a bus with some high school classmates and an older boy grabs my hair from behind and pulls it up. It's impossible for me to turn my head.

I whisper, stunned. "What are you doing?"

"Giddy up, horsey. Horsey!"

"Stop it!"

The bus slows for a red light. The boys are oohing and aahing at a hot car revving below us. They are way more impressed by motor horsepower than me, so the guy lets go.

I do not look back at him or unfasten my ponytail or gather my hair in my own hand. My friend suggests changing seats, but I refuse. My head and neck prickle from pain, the shock, the violence, yet I won't let anyone see it. At fourteen, I feel shame seep into my chest, my stomach.

I didn't understand, the week before, when a friend of my mother exclaimed, "Look at you, blooming before our eyes!" Then, I felt confused and uncomfortable. But on the bus, I get it. I'm not a girl anymore, I'm a "young woman" and everybody evidently knows, but I have no idea what that means. The day before at our lockers, my friend remarked that my hair needed brushing—untamed, tangled, forgotten in the morning rush out the door. But neatly in a ponytail, my hair, like my womanhood, is a liability. A hazard. A risk.

I do not want to be yanked by my hair or called a horse for anyone's lame joke again, so the next time I ride on the bus, I tuck my hair under my jacket. Or divide it at the back and settle the two handfuls to the front. For years.

In my first semester of university, I accompany a friend to a varsity football game, and she gets us invited to the team party after, on campus. There are other girls there, coupled up with players, but older than us. Some, like me, have natural hair and baby-oiled eyelids. The quarterback, in his leather-sleeved team Melton, laughs with the others but keeps glancing over at me. When my friend, who wants to leave, starts leading me to the door, the guy steps between us, eyes on me and holds up a plastic beer glass.

"If you come to the after-party, I can drive you home later."

I grin. "I thought this was the after-party."

He doesn't laugh. "This is the pre-party. We go for pizza next."

My friend says bye and the quarterback's hand is at home on my back. We stand watching the others and the others watch us.

It was my first football game, I say, and I talk about music, my piano practising schedule which, besides classes, is all I normally do. Never have I said yes to a spontaneous after-party with a random guy, even if he is the captain of tonight's winning football team, but I don't reveal that. He finishes his beer and gives the signal to go for pizza and everyone does.

He drives a red sportscar. Not new, but his, he tells me, and he enjoys driving it, especially on the curves. He takes a circuitous route to the pizza place, over the river and back. I wonder if the reason for the longer back-and-forth drive is to have more time to talk, especially since he doesn't turn on the radio, but he concentrates on tight cornering, so I remain silent. Maybe he's lost, like me when I navigate the many branching roads and bridges of the river valley. For several minutes, I feel unsafe, as if he might take me somewhere else to assault me. The prickles on my neck rise again. But the red car arrives at the appointed spot first, we push together tables for the others, and everyone eats pizza at midnight. The guys talk over each other, still deconstructing the game. The girls sip their drinks, glance at each other, but they are unable to converse over the loud play-by-play. I don't listen either.

When I ask to go home, the drive to my house is direct, he says he'll call, and he does.

The date is a movie, his pick. I'm a little startled by his choice.

"I don't usually go to restricted ones." I'm not yet eighteen but do not explain that I was accelerated in school. He's a fourth-year student with a limited course load during football season.

"The guys said it was good." He plants one on my lips before we get out of the car. I am aware that he and the guys, who aren't even there, are in charge. In the theatre, his arm around my shoulders, he winds my hair, loose and freshly washed, in his fingers. Sometimes, he grasps a whole handful. Urgent.

I don't like the movie. A faux western. A girl is strapped down on railway ties, shirt torn open, breasts exposed, her nipples pinched, hard, by the sweaty sunburnt actor standing over her. The girl is gagged. Her horse is shot. Screams muffled. I wonder if this why the guys like it.

After we leave the empty theatre and reach the dim hallway, he pushes me against the wall and pins me there while he explores my mouth with his tongue. I'm surprised. And resist the best I can. I wipe off my mouth.

He drives me home, quiet as usual. I wish he would say something because the frightening images from the movie are flashing, imprinting onto my memory, and I would rather talk, but so far all we have in common is a rotten film.

He walks me to my gate. I back away slightly even though he does not attempt another sloppy kiss. I say, "Thanks."

"Bye," he says. "No sense kicking a dead horse."

But I feel the kicks over and over. The teen on the bus, the quarterback, the violent dude in the western (the actor is later charged with partner abuse, I notice). That night and for many nights after, the images haunt me periodically, especially when I'm stressed, sick, hurt, or tired.

A faceless "he" is there, hands pulling, twisting my hair, pinching. For decades.

Forty-five years later, I am upset and fed up that the images of pinching and pulling still bother me. My daughters have grown and left home. My husband has retired. My father has died.

I grant myself time to grieve, and the grieving lets me look for a route to healing. I take not a linear path, but a spiral one. Straight-line point-to-point thinking is direct, but more vulnerable to interruption, like a stop sign or a flat tire. I try spiral thinking, a feminine and artistic form of thought, arising from creative and critical tension, circling and layering and sometimes magical, asking, "what if." I picture the generative double-helix of DNA. Spiral thinking is elastic and easily circles back for another point of view, improvises and promotes problem-solving, creation, survival. Gently, I tug on a tendril.

I Google "girl tied on a railway." I watch a film clip from 1948, a damsel in distress staring down a long, straight train track loaded with dynamite, about to be run over by an iron horse at full speed. Close-up on the woman, hair mussed and clothing akimbo, gagged so she can't scream, then a long shot of the train loaded with raw logs coming around the mountain. As the railway is blown up, the narrator, a buoyant male voice, says, "There goes the trestle. And the girl. Then the cargo of wooden gold. What a mess to clean up before supper!" The woman in the film is secondary to the timber being pulled by the train and falling down the valley on top of her. Expendable, while the logs will be retrieved for their great value.

In this scenario, I wonder who is making supper.

Suddenly, I recognize the male fantasy: a fake trestle and toy train in an old film stunt of a vicious attack on a woman's body. I realize that my long-ago bad date and longer-ago scary bus ride belong to the same outdated male fantasy, which has no place in my imagination, I decide, and therefore has no power over me, not anymore.

The sensation is epiphanic, like in the moment I discerned that the crouching bear on the path at dusk was a boulder. Or once, postpartum, plagued by dark thoughts, I found the Latin word for what I felt, and my malaise soon faded away. This time, images of hair-pulling and nipple-pinching are properly categorized by my brain, and drop, dissolve, and disappear as if I were scrubbing years of dirt from a pot. The work feels good, and my mind clears.

Months later, the pot stays clean.

I wonder why this process has taken so long. I suspect a compilation of factors led to this revelation: time studying literary tropes, the advancement of the internet, my own hormone changes, the warp of pandemic time, loss, and the conscious effort of rebalancing. My father's generous spirit, perhaps, guides me.

I ask myself why other bad dates, dangerous situations, and difficulties never affected me like this dirt I finally, successfully, scoured off. Possibly, those first offensive images lingered so long because they happened before I learned to use research, imagination, and curation to transform experience into new stories of my own.

Even though I am not her anymore, I mourn for the unease of the younger me.

Yet I am in awe of the image drop by my senior self. Grateful for the disruption, I wonder if this is what aging can do. I welcome its wisdom.

I untie the woman on the railway and pull her up, off the tracks, onto a path of her own. Face the sunset together. Don't need a horse. Wear our hair long.

Back to the Page

Ellen Kartz

For as long as I can remember, what I most wanted to do was write. There was a brief period in my pre-teen years when I thought about becoming a musician as I first discovered the magic contained on the fretboard of my father's Yamaha acoustic guitar. In my late teens, I was cross-cast as a male bank robber in a friend's Edmonton Fringe play and that had me considering a life on the stage. I even spent my first years at university pursuing an undergraduate degree in drama.

But I always came back to the page. It's not my only artistic love, but it is the artistic love of my life.

I'm maybe nine years old in the Strathcona County Library. I love the smell of the books, the quiet between the rows of shelves in the adult books section. I love the forest green carpet, the overhead fluorescent lights. I am allowed three books today. I know which row I want to visit. I drag the stool over; the books I'm after are on the top shelf. The stool is metal, round. It depresses as I step up, making an embarrassing screech as it settles under me.

I stand on tiptoes, reach high above my head. I hook a finger over one of the thick spines and tip it toward me. I hope I am strong enough to catch it before it tumbles to the ground. The book slides into my hands. The cover is deep blue fabric with gold embossed letters. *The Collected Works of William Wordsworth*.

I open the book and run my fingers over the words pressed into the pages. The words are strange. I try to sound them out silently in my head as I feel them on the page.

It's like Braille, I think, as the imprints of letters pass beneath the tips of my fingers.

I'm too young to understand the poetry, but what I do understand is its music. I sound out the words, catch the scent lifting from the old pages, feel the typeface beneath my hands.

The overhead lights dim for a moment. The library is closing. I need to find Mom. I'll take only one book today. It will have to be enough.

My mother told me once that I used to play Bookstore as a kid. I'd bring my books out to the living room, line them up on the couches and affix price tags to the covers. She would pretend to be a customer who was coming in to buy books. I don't remember doing this, but I don't doubt that it's true. It sounds exactly like something I'd do.

When I was twenty-seven, I moved back home to Edmonton after finishing my undergrad degree in Calgary. It was difficult to move home after living on my own in another city for four years. To help ease the transition back, I decided to take some time in the first months to focus on writing. I was going to extend my final university creative writing project into a novel-in-verse. I spent the summer working on the book and, during that time, learned I'd won a writing contest at Mount Royal University.

It's a crisp fall morning. Mom is back in the hospital for another operation. She and I are waiting in her room for an orderly to take her down to the OR. I was away at school in Calgary the first time she got sick, so the wait is new for me. I pace the room, watch the sky out the window, the parking lot below.

Her surgeon, Dr. Hanson, arrives for a pre-surgical pep talk.

"I don't want you to worry about anything," he says, patting Mom's arm. "We're just going in to remove a blockage. We're not even looking for cancer. I don't want you to worry about a thing."

He leaves the room and Mom bolts upright.

"I have to turn my life around," she says.

Dad had moved out the same week I moved home a few months earlier. Through the summer, Mom had spent most of her time in bed, watching television in the dark. She blamed herself for the breakup of their marriage.

"I have to," she says. "I just *have* to."

"Then you will," I tell her.

"You think so?"

"Of course. I think you can do it. I believe in you."

She starts to cry.

"Thank you," she says.

"I mean it. If there's anything you need, anything at all, I'm here for you, Mom."

"That means a lot," she says through tears.

"Just go a step at a time."

"Baby steps, right?"

It's something we've said to each other since I first moved to Calgary. One of my professors had talked about life not being a series of great leaps, but a progression of small steps.

"You can't tackle the whole mountain at once," he'd said. "It's just too big."

I smile at Mom.

"Yeah. Baby steps."

The orderly arrives to take her down to surgery and I walk with them as far as they let me go.

"I'll be waiting for you when you get out," I say.

The results of Mom's surgery revealed that her cancer had come back and had spread throughout her abdomen. Her condition was terminal. She ended up back in the hospital after having a stroke on Christmas Eve. I spent that winter and the following spring helping care for her in hospital until she passed away in early May, two weeks before my twenty-eighth birthday.

I'm now thirty-four. It's five in the morning when I open the email from the University of British Columbia. They are writing to notify me of my acceptance into their optional-residency MFA in Creative Writing. I stare at the computer screen until the words become real.

I dial Dad's number, knowing he'll be up, getting ready to leave to work.

"Dad! I got in! I'm going to grad school!"

I decided to take a break from writing after completing my master's degree. I was going to wait a year and then continue to work on my thesis—a book of linked nonfiction stories about growing up on the acreage, summers spent at Grandma's cabin, all culminating with the story of Mom's death. It had been a difficult book to write, and by the end of my thesis year I felt like I'd been sent away to live on the moon. I needed to spend some time back on Earth.

I was attending an event for the Edmonton Poetry Festival one night when I met *her*. She stared through me across the table in the dimly lit venue. As we chatted, the room fell away under her stare. Later, she asked me to dinner.

What began as a look across a table stretched into four years of intense verbal and emotional abuse.

I'm forty-two now, although it's sometimes hard to remember—I feel ninety. It's late and I'm very drunk, self-medicating with vodka and beer in front of my computer screen. It's the only way I can sleep. Otherwise, the hamster in my head runs circles all night.

I open a folder on my desktop marked "Writing." It holds everything, including my thesis. It's been years since I last looked at it.

Do I dare?

What the hell.

I click on the document and wait for Word to come to life. I stare at the title page and think about the year I spent writing it. I scroll through the table of contents, the acknowledgements, the dedication, to the opening story. It's a recollection of the time I took all the bad reminders of my childhood and burned them in the fire pit at my grandmother's lake cabin—clothes, letters, Girl Guide uniforms. The next morning, I scooped the ashes into a box and took them home to bury in the acreage backyard, far at the end, behind the row of willow trees.

I keep scrolling through the document until I come to the story of Mom's death. It brings it all back—the tedium of hospital time, the seizures, the endless parade of medications, the smell of sickness, her inevitable deterioration. It's intense, yet unsentimental. Before I know it, I'm in tears.

"My god," I say to the screen, "what a thing to have lived through."

I'm inside and outside the narrative at the same time—remembering it, but also its audience. I know what the narrator was thinking, feeling, but it's someone else's story, too, from another lifetime, when I cared so much. How could that year have been better than this one?

The answer that comes is not what I expect—because I knew that one was going to end.

After I got out of that relationship, it took a year before I started to feel like myself again. To help build myself back up, I planned and trained for a trek in Nepal to Mount Everest Base Camp. Two years later, in 2018, I wrote, produced, and acted in a one-person stage show based on that trip. As I stepped off the stage following the performance, I saw my father in the audience and caught his eye. He was on his feet with everyone else, steadying himself with the handles of his walker; his eyes were filled with pride.

It's early 2020, and for the past five years I have been working for a non-profit organization that supports Alberta writers. This is when the first news reports come in about an illness from Asia spreading across the globe.

The news shifts to announce the first recorded deaths and lockdowns in China. The death toll begins to rise. Johns Hopkins University's website posts a map charting the worldwide growth of the virus. The map tracks rates of infection, numbers of survivors, how many have died. Each day, the world map fills with larger and larger red circles.

I begin receiving emails from other organizations announcing event cancellations. More of those same messages come in each day.

One morning, my boss sits down on a chair in the centre of our office at a staff meeting and looks around the room.

"Well," she says, "what does everyone think? They haven't issued a work from home order yet, but they're talking about it. Should we close the office and all start working remotely?"

At the time the pandemic hit, I had managed to extend the story I'd written for the show in 2018 into a book-length manuscript. It was still a few drafts from being submittable but was close to being ready to go to an editor. I had also applied for a grant to start a small poetry chapbook press and found out later in the year that the grant application had been accepted. Just when it felt like things were coming together again, the whole world went into mourning.

The phone wakes me at five in the morning on Christmas Eve. It's my sister. She and her husband have decided to drive to Edmonton. Dad suffered a heart attack earlier in the week and has been isolated in the ICU for the past couple of days.

"Am I crazy to rush back?" my sister asks.

"No," I tell her. "Either he's going to get out of the hospital and we're going to need to decide where to place him, or he's not going to get out and you'll never forgive yourself for not coming."

Later that morning, the phone rings again. This time it's the hospital, asking if I can get in touch with Dad's partner and come down to the

ICU. With my brother living in Kelowna and my sister in Nanaimo, I'm the only one left to call.

I arrive at the Royal Alex and meet Dad's partner at the ground level doors. We have to go through screening to be let in. Normally teeming with patients, staff and visitors, The Alex is nearly empty as we make our way up to the fourth floor.

They kit us up before we are allowed to enter the room—masks, gloves, gowns, face shields. I look around me—the ICU has become a war zone. Hospital equipment fills the halls and garbage bins overflow with used gowns, gloves and masks.

The man in the bed looks like my father, but the man in the bed is no longer a man. He is a body being kept alive by a machine that fills his lungs with air.

I touch his hand. It's cold. The room is cold. Despite the temperature, sweat runs down my back.

"The head of the ICU is with another patient right now," Dad's nurse tells us. "He should be here soon."

Two hours go by before the glass door to Dad's room slides open again and a man enters.

"Hello. I am Dr. Mishra," he tells us. "Thank you both for coming in."

He leans down and looks me in the eye.

"How *are* you today?" he asks.

I glance at the bed.

"As well as can be expected," I say.

Behind his mask, Dr. Mishra smiles.

He walks over to the bed and begins to tell us what I already know inside. Dad suffered a massive heart attack. They worked for half an hour to revive him. They had stopped chest compressions and were about to declare him dead when his pulse started again.

"If I had it to do over," Dr Mishra says, "I would have let him go. With his age and the advanced stage of his condition, there's no chance of meaningful recovery."

We'll have to take him off the ventilator. They are short on beds, so a decision needs to be made quickly.

"My sister is on her way here from Nanaimo. Can we wait for her?" I ask.

"When is she supposed to get here?"

"About ten o'clock tonight."

"I'll check and see."

Dad died just before midnight on Christmas Eve in 2020. He had been living with a degenerative brain condition for seven years before his death.

My sister and her husband drove from their front door straight to the hospital that day. I called my brother from Dad's room and Dad's partner held the phone up to his ear so my brother could say goodbye. Because of the continual outbreaks of the virus, we had to wait to hold the funeral. In the fall of 2022, we finally said goodbye as a family.

It is now June of 2023, and I am nearing the age my mother was when she died. I've been counting down the years since I was twenty-seven. I still work as an arts administrator for that provincial writing organization, helping Alberta writers promote their work or take steps toward accomplishing their dreams. It's enjoyable work, fulfills some of what I felt as a kid while poring over Wordsworth, Whitman, Dickinson. But it's not the same as writing.

Every few years, I find myself positioned to move a few steps closer to fulfilling my own dreams, and right now I find myself there again. I finished that manuscript and have started sending it out. I have plans for two more. It's time again to write. It's time to bring writing to the centre of my life. And there will be no more interruptions.

Endnotes

1. Writing the personal essay "When did you lose the power of speech?" is what first sparked Rona Altrows's interest in co-curating and co-editing, with Uchechukwu Umezurike, this anthology on interruption. The essay first appeared in *Standing Up: An Anthology for Ukraine*, edited by Marion Lougheed with Bruce Lilly, Off Topic Publishing 2023.

2. In Thea Bowering's short story *Quicksilver*, words by Lucia Joyce, quoted by the character Aisling, come from a recorded session between Lucia and her psychologist quoted in Carol Loeb Shloss's biography *Lucia Joyce: To Dance in the Wake* (New York, NY: Picador, 2003). The writer borrowed the half-line like *the tender fire of stars*, and paraphrased adjacent lines, from James Joyce's story "The Dead," in *Dubliners*. The half-line *The ghost of something strange* and guilty is from Charles Baudelaire's poem "Une Martyre," translated as "Murdered Woman" by Edna St. Vincent Millay in *Flowers of Evil* (New York, NY: Harper, 1936).

Contributors

ADEMOLA ADESOLA is an Assistant Professor of Postcolonial Studies at the Department of English, Languages, and Cultures, Mount Royal University, Calgary, Canada. Ademola's research and teaching interests are postcolonial literatures, African/Black Diaspora literatures, child soldier narratives, war and literature, popular culture, and human rights issues. Ademola has published essays and book chapters on African literature and sociopolitical issues. One of Ademola's scholarly projects is representations of child soldiers in contemporary African narratives.

SCOTT ALDERSON was born in Edmonton and resides in Calgary. He has nine books in print as well as a DVD (Three and a Half Poets Stir the Soul of Cowtown, Sweetgrass Films, 2008). He has been President of Three Small White Mice Publications since 2001. He has eleven YouTube Videos (Scott Alderson Poetry). He identifies as a Street Poet, and what he lacks in formal training, he makes up for in his passion for poetry.

RONA ALTROWS is a Canadian writer, editor, and playwright. She is the 2025 winner of the Prairie Grindstone Prize, awarded for her body of work and commitment to supporting both emerging and established writers. Her books of short fiction include *A Run on Hose*, which won the W.O. Mitchell Book Prize, *Key in Lock*, and *At This Juncture*. She has edited or co-edited three previous anthologies, *You Look Good for Your Age*, *Waiting* (with Julie Sedivy), and *Shy* (with Naomi K. Lewis), all published by The University of Alberta Press. Her book of personal essays, *Anxious Kid Makes Pretty Good*, will be published by Now or Never Publishing in fall, 2026.

DUSTIN ARCHIBALD writes stories for children, teens, and adults, although his current focus is on pre/teen books especially with the Asha Anderson series. When he's not writing he edits books and takes care of foster cats. He lives in Grande Prairie, Alberta, Canada with his wife, Tracy, and son, Logan.Thea Bowering's collection of short fiction Love at Last Sight (NeWest Press) focuses on the figure of the female flâneur. It won the Alberta Book Publishing Award for Trade Fiction Book of the Year and was longlisted for The Alberta Readers' Choice Award in 2014. In 2022 she was Artist in Residence at Yorath House, Edmonton. In 2023 she received an Edmonton Arts Council grant to research her Finnish family history on Quadra Island, BC, towards several writing projects, including a novel based on her mother's life in the 1960s experimental arts scenes in Canada.

MONI BRAR (she/her) comes from a long lineage of illiterate subsistence farmers and spends her time contemplating land, loss, language, and longing. Her creative work aims to open space for class, gender, and racial equity. She is the winner of writing awards from *Grain*, *The Fiddlehead, PRISM, Room, CV2, and The Ex-Puritan.* Her work appears in *Best Canadian Poetry* (Biblioasis), *The Literary Review of Canada, Passages North,* and elsewhere. She believes art contains the possibility of healing.

JENNA BUTLER (she/her) is an award-winning poet, essayist, editor, and professor of creative and environmental writing. She is the author of three books of poetry, two collections of ecological essays, and an Arctic travelogue. *Revery: A Year of Bees,* essays about beekeeping, the climate crisis, and trauma recovery, was a finalist for the 2021 Governor General's Literary Award in Non-Fiction and a longlisted title for CBC Canada Reads 2023. An off-grid organic farmer in northern Treaty 6, Butler is grateful to have the opportunity to help support diverse communities of growers and reciprocal relationships to the land.

ALISON CLARKE is a poet, fantasy author, and visual artist who is also the Amazon #1 bestselling author of *Phillis: A Poetry Collection* (University of Calgary Press, 2020), and the award-winning young adult fantasy trilogy, *The Sisterhood*, for which she won the Diversity Magazine award for 2016 Writer of the Year. She has also won the 2020 Fil Fraser award for her contributions to literary and visual art. Alison was the 2021 Writer in Residence of the Alexandra Writers' Centre. Alison believes that stories can change the world.

MEGHAN EAKER (they/them) is a queer, non-binary, mixed nehiyaw & white amiskwaciywaskahikan-based poet and member of the Woodland Cree First Nation. They are a PhD student in Indigenous Studies at the University of Alberta studying nehiyaw storytelling as a creative practice towards miyo pimatisiwin (a good life).

LUCIANA ERREGUE-SACCHI is an Argentinian Canadian award-winning publisher (Laberinto Press), a writer, translator, and art historian. Her work has been long-listed for the Susan Crean Award. Her debut chapbook, *Of Mothers and Madonnas* (Polyglot) launched in 2023.

KUFRE FRIESENHAN is a mother and has a PhD from the Department of English and Film Studies, University of Alberta. Her research interests include oral literatures, petroculture, feminist studies, Indigenous literatures, and trauma studies. Her research was supported by the Social Sciences and Humanities Research Council (SSHRC).

SAMANTHA JONES (she/her) is a writer, copyeditor, and earth scientist based in Moh'kins'tsis (Calgary, Alberta) on the traditional territory of Treaty 7 peoples and the home of Métis Nation of Alberta, Districts 5 and 6. She is a magazine and journal enthusiast with work published in *Room*, *CV2*, *Grain*, *THIS*, *GeoHumanities*, *Arctic*, *EVENT*, *The Capilano Review*, and elsewhere. Her visual OCD poetry chapbook, *Site Orientation*, was published by the Blasted Tree in 2022. Sam is proud of her mixed heritage, which is Black Canadian and white settler. Her poetry collection, *Attic Rain*, is out with NeWest Press.

CLARA A. B. JOSEPH is the author of the long poem, *The Face of the Other* (IP, Brisbane 2016), and the collections of poems, *Dandelions for Bhabha* (IP, Brisbane 2018) and *M/OTHER* (Wipf and Stock, 2024). Her poems have appeared in publications of the League of Canadian Poets and journals such as *Literature and Aesthetics, RCLAS E-Zine, S/tick, Canadian Woman Studies, Prosopisia: An International Journal of Poetry & Creative Writing, Mother Earth International*, and *Toronto Review*. She is a professor of English and adjunct professor of Religious Studies at the University of Calgary.

ELLEN KARTZ (she/her) is a poet and nonfiction writer living in Edmonton. She holds a Master of Fine Arts in Creative Writing from the University of British Columbia and a professional writing certificate from Mount Royal University. In 2018, she self-produced a one-person stage show and poetry chapbook, both titled *The Tenderness of Stone* about a trek she made in 2016 through Nepal's Khumbu Valley to Mount Everest Base Camp. In 2020, Ellen founded Armistice Press and launched a quartet of chapbooks by emerging queer Edmonton authors. Currently, she is a mentor with the Writers' Guild of Alberta's Horizons Writing Circle while on sabbatical to focus on her writing.

KELLY KAUR grew up in Singapore and lives in Calgary. Her first novel is *Letters to Singapore*. Her poem and essay were awarded Honorable Mention in the Creators of Justice Literary Awards, New York, and nominated for a Pushcart Prize. Kelly is a Preliminary Reader and judged 2 projects for the International Human Rights Arts Movement (*IHRAM)*, New York. She curated/edited *From Africa with Love: Voices of a Creative Continent,* for *IHRAM*. Her works are going to the moon in 2024 in the

NOVA and Polaris collection. Her children's book, *Howdy, I'm Harnam Singh,* is out with Red Barn Books Inc.

YEJIDE KILANKO was born in Ibadan, Nigeria and lives in Ontario, Canada. She writes poetry and fiction. Kilanko's debut novel, *Daughters Who Walk This Path*, a 2012 Canadian national bestseller, was long-listed for the 2016 Nigeria Prize for Literature. Her short fiction is in the anthology, *New Orleans Review 2017: The African Literary Hustle*. Kilanko's latest novel, *A Good Name*, was published in 2021 while her short story, *This Tangible Thing*, was shortlisted for the 2023 Caine Prize. Her next book, *In Our Own Ways*, is forthcoming in 2025. A therapist in children's mental health, Kilanko also writes children's picture books.

KATHERINE KOLLER writes for stage, screen and page. Her books are *Voices of the Land: The Seed Savers and Other Plays, Art Lessons* (novel) and *Winning Chance* (stories), which won a High Plains Book Award. Short fiction has also been published in *Grain, Room, Epiphany, Alberta Views, Very Much Alive, Polish[ed], LitSphere* and *Edify*, and creative nonfiction in *Prairie Journal, The Pandemic and Me,* and *WestWord*. She is a founding producer of Edmonton Script Salon, a monthly new play reading series now in its tenth year, and a current member of the Citadel Theatre Playwrights' Lab.

MICHELINE MAYLOR-KOVITZ was Calgary's Poet Laureate 2016-18. Her latest poetry collection *The Bad Wife* (2021) won the BPAA Raymond Souster Award for best poetry in Alberta. Her previous collection *Little Wildheart* (U of Alberta Press))was long listed for both the Pat Lowther and Raymond Souster awards. She recently won Queen's Platinum Jubilee Award for literary contributions to Alberta in 2022 and the Lois Hole Award for Editorial Excellence in Alberta. Her work has been recently translated into Farsi, Chinese, and Italian.

WENDY MCGRATH is the winner of the inaugural Prairie Grindstone Prize. A Métis poet, writer, and artist living in amiskwacîwâskahikan (Edmonton), McGrath's writing embraces multiple genres. Her most recent publication, *The Orange Scribbler* (Jack Pine 2023) is a chapbook/artist's book inspired by heirloom recipes. She has collaborated with visual artists and musicians, exploring the relationships between genres. Her latest collaboration, *The Beauty of Vultures*, (forthcoming NeWest Press 2025) is a poetry collection inspired by and including the bird/wildlife photography of Danny Mile. McGrath has published four novels, two poetry collections, and two chapbooks/artist's books which explore a range of forms and approaches.

MARCO MELFI won *The Fiddlehead's 2021 Ralph Gustafson Poetry Contest* and has had poems published in *Arc Poetry Magazine*, *EVENT*, *The Literary Review of Canada*, *PRISM*, *The Antigonish Review*, *The New Quarterly*, and *Prairie Fire*. His chapbook, *In between trains*, was published in 2014. He lives in Edmonton on Treaty 6 Territory.

SHAZIA HAFIZ RAMJI is the author of *Port of Being*, a finalist for the 2019 Vancouver Book Award, the Gerald Lampert Poetry Award, the BC Book Prizes, and the winner of the Robert Kroetsch Award for Innovative Poetry. Her poetry has been anthologized twice in *The Best Canadian Poetry* and shortlisted twice for the National Magazine Awards. Her writing has appeared in the 2022 Montreal International Poetry Prize anthology, *The Malahat Review*, and *The Literary Review of Canada*. She lives in western Canada and London, UK.

ALEX RETTIE writes from Calgary. His poems have been published in journals in Canada, the US, and the UK, have been featured at Calgary's Fairy Tales Film Festival (2022) and in the short film *Old Dragon Man* (2024). He is the recipient of a 2023 project grant from Calgary Arts Development, which he is using to complete his first poetry manuscript.

GINA ROITMAN is an author, biographer, and writing coach. who lives in Montreal. Her latest work is the literary novel, *Don't Ask* and the collection *Tell Me a Story, Tell Me the Truth*. Her essays, short stories, and poems have appeared in numerous anthologies including *The New Spice Box*, *Wherever I Find Myself*, and *Poetica*. She was also the subject of the award-winning documentary, *My Mother, the Nazi Midwife and Me*. Since 2018, Gina has led ongoing, memoir-writing workshops for The Generations After of Washington, DC. whose work has been collected into an anthology: *Missing Pieces: Growing Up in the Shadow of the Shoah*.

LENORE ROWNTREE lives in Vancouver. Her linked collection of stories *See You Later Maybe Never* was a finalist for a Sunshine Coast Writers Award. Her novel *Cluck* was a finalist in The Great BC Novel Contest. She is lead editor and contributor to the anthology *Hidden Lives: true stories from people who live with mental illness*. Her poetry has been included in *The Best of the Best of Canadian Poetry*. Her essays have been shortlisted for a CBC nonfiction award. She is a contributor to many magazines and newspapers including *Geist* and *The Globe & Mail*.

JIDE SALAWU is a Nigerian writer who lives in Canada, and the author of *Preface for Leaving Homeland* published under the African Poetry Book Fund. He also co-edited (with Rasaq Malik) *African Urban Echoes* (a poetry anthology on African cities), now out with Griots Lounge Canada.

ANNA MARIE SEWELL is the author of *Humane* (2020) and *Urbane* (2023) (novels, Stonehouse Publishing); *For the Changing Moon*: Poems & Songs (Thistledown Press, 2018), and Fifth World Drum (poetry, Frontenac House, 2009); lyricist for choral scores *At First Light* (2023, Hinshaw Music) and *Journey Song* (2022, Cypress Music). She was Edmonton's 4th Poet Laureate. Her artistic practice features multidisciplinary, intercultural collaborations, and work as a cultural educator. Honouring her Mi'gmaq/Anishinaabe/Polish heritage, she creates resources for formal and community educational initiatives including Japan's Peace Boat. Ms Sewell lives in Amiskwaciy/Edmonton, and posts at prairiepomes.com

MADELAINE SHAW-WONG writes fiction and non-fiction, novels and short stories, and occasionally dabbles in poetry. Madelaine's writing often revolves around the theme of family, their troubles and complex relationships. In addition to her self-published books, her stories have appeared in several literary journals including *Freefall* and *Mused,* and in anthologies. Her passion for travel has taken her to many beautiful locations around the world, but mostly, she can be found at home at her keyboard, hammering out another story. Her works-in-progress involve magic, ghosts, and of course, family.

UCHECHUKWU PETER UMEZURIKE is an Assistant Professor in the Department of English, the 2025-2026 Wayne O. McCready Emerging Fellow at the Calgary Institute for the Humanities, University of Calgary, Canada and the winner of the 2025 African Literature Association's Best Book Award (Creative Writing). He is the author of *there's more*, *Double Wahala, Double Trouble*, *Wish Maker*, and a co-editor of *Wreaths for a Wayfarer*. His monograph, *Masculinity in Nigerian Fiction: Receptivity and Gender,* is forthcoming from Edinburgh University Press in November 2025.

GIAN MARCO VISCONTI is an Arbëreshë and South Asian Canadian poet, born and raised in Edmonton, Alberta. He received the Glass Buffalo English Poetry Prize in 2016 and the SAAG Writing Prize in 2019. He was longlisted for the CBC Poetry Prize in 2018 and a finalist for the Alberta Magazine Award for Poetry in 2023. Gian Marco writes in English while weaving elements of his heritage languages (Italian, Gujarati, and Arabic) into his poetic work. He holds a Master of Library

& Information Studies from the University of Alberta and a Master of Planning from the University of Calgary.

TERESA WOUTERS is an educator, entertainer, and entrepreneur. She is a multi-published, award-winning author of many short pieces and poems. Her first published novel, *Creeboy*, has made its way on many Readers' choice long lists and onto provincial school curricula for novel studies. The second novel in the Creeboy trilogy, which is coming soon to bookshelves near you, is called *Oskayak*.

Photo Credit: Lucy Altrows

About the Editors

RONA ALTROWS is a Canadian writer, editor, and playwright. She is the 2025 winner of the Prairie Grindstone Prize, awarded for her body of work and commitment to supporting both emerging and established writers. Her books of short fiction include *A Run on Hose*, which won the W.O. Mitchell Book Prize, *Key in Lock*, and *At This Juncture*. She has edited or co-edited three previous anthologies, *You Look Good for Your Age*, *Waiting* (with Julie Sedivy), and *Shy* (with Naomi K. Lewis), all published by The University of Alberta Press. Her book of personal essays, *Anxious Kid Makes Pretty Good*, will be published by Now or Never Publishing in fall, 2026.

UCHECHUKWU PETER UMEZURIKE is an Assistant Professor in the Department of English, the 2025-2026 Wayne O. McCready Emerging Fellow at the Calgary Institute for the Humanities, University of Calgary, Canada and the winner of the 2025 African Literature Association's Best Book Award (Creative Writing). He is the author of *there's more*, *Double Wahala, Double Trouble*, *Wish Maker*, and a co-editor of *Wreaths for a Wayfarer*. His monograph, *Masculinity in Nigerian Fiction: Receptivity and Gender*, is forthcoming from Edinburgh University Press in November 2025.